# Intermediate States
## A Nonfiction Anthology
## The Anomalist 13

## Edited by
## Patrick Huyghe and Dennis Stacy

Anomalist Books
San Antonio * New York

Original Publication of ANOMALIST BOOKS

*Intermediate States: The Anomalist 13*
Copyright © 2007 by Patrick Huyghe and Dennis Stacy
ISBN: 1933665262

Cover image from Bartholomeo Eustachi's *Tabulae anatomicae*,
1783, courtesy of the National Library of Medicine.
Book design by Seale Studios

Anomalist Books            Anomalist Books
5150 Broadway #108         PO Box 577
San Antonio, TX 78209      Jefferson Valley, NY 10535

# CONTENTS

*Between official facts and public fantasies…*

# SUSPENSION OF DISBELIEF:
## THE GREAT YARMOUTH BRIDGE DISASTER OF 1845
### BY JOHN REPPION

YARMOUTH SUSPENSION BRIDGE,
AS IT APPEARED AFTER THE ACCIDENT, BY WHICH 79 LIVES WERE LOST,
ON FRIDAY EVENING MAY 2, 1845.

In late 2005 my wife caught the family tree bug and set about researching her ancestry. In addition to trawling online archives of births, deaths, and marriages, as well as censuses and military records, she also managed to amass a large collection of photographs, clippings, and even a few older relatives' previous attempts at family trees. Amongst this seemingly ever-expanding genealogical archive we came across a newspaper article entitled "The Suspension Bridge Disaster. Memories of a Yarmouth Old Lady [-] Her Narrow Escape." My wife's curiosity was not held for long as she had seen the clipping before. Indeed, I myself had already heard of the Bridge Disaster via my mother-in-law. However, after reading the old article in full, I realized that I had not previously appreciated the extreme peculiarity of the event.

The clipping was taken from a Great Yarmouth, UK newspaper entitled *The Mercury*, published (we may assume from the evidence) in 1927. The subject of the article is an interview with ninety-two year old local resident Mrs. Sarah Bentall, sister of Captain Bammant who was the onetime harbormaster of Yarmouth, and my wife's great, great, great aunt. In the piece Mrs. Bentall is asked to recount her memories of the area and its history. Her most vivid recollection is of the 2nd of May 1845, the day the Yarmouth Suspension Bridge collapsed.

"As she reminded us, a clown, performing in Yarmouth Theatre at that time, had declared his intention of making the journey from the Haven Bridge to the Suspension Bridge in a tub drawn by six white geese, guided by scarlet reigns."

The clown's name was Nelson and his improbable journey was the cause of a disaster of quite remarkable proportions.

In the article, Mrs. Bentall explains how she would have been around ten years old at the time and had attended the scene accompanied by her two sisters and her aunt. Many people had gathered at the bridge in anticipation of seeing the buffoon complete his voyage.

"Someone shouted, 'Here he comes!' and the geese could just be seen coming around the bend of the river. People rushed to the side of the bridge and all at once there was a loud alarming crack."

Mrs. Bentall was able to pull her younger sister Harriet to safety just before the bridge gave way under the weight of the accumulated throng. Around four hundred people plunged into the river and of those more than seventy were drowned, "mostly the children of trades people who had been taken down to see the sight. Some parents lost all their children."

Also found amongst my wife's ample archive was second photocopied newspaper clipping, this one from "Jeremy Beadle's Today's The Day," *The Daily Express,* May 2, 1980, which corroborates the story's key elements whilst omitting the death count (presumably in an effort to make the occurrence seem light hearted and humorous): "In a washtub drawn by geese a clown sailed up the river in Great Yarmouth today in 1845. 400 spectators followed him into the river when a bridge collapsed!"

Further evidence of the bizarre tragedy can be found, as one might expect, upon the graves of the victims themselves. George Beloe was nine years old when he was drowned in the catastrophe and an image of a twisted and broken bridge can still be seen engraved upon his tombstone in Saint Nicholas's churchyard in Yarmouth.

• • •

The reality of *The Yarmouth Suspension Bridge Disaster*, the largest peacetime tragedy ever to have befallen the town is, it seems, unquestionable, but what of the mysterious fool who caused the events of that day? What of Nelson the clown and his goose powered voyage?

The name of Nelson was attributed to the entertainer in only one source (other than the aforementioned clipping) that I could find; the July 2005 edition of a magician's E-zine entitled *Top Hat* quoting its source as "an old newspaper cutting dating back to May 1[9]29" and located in Yarmouth's library archive. Nelson still seems an odd choice of name to me, and given the close ties that Lord Nelson had with the port of Yarmouth it appears almost disrespectful. Of course, it is entirely possible that I am underestimating the comedic value of "Nelson" sailing up the river in a washtub and it is feasible that the moniker was chosen for that very reason.

Searching the internet for evidence of goose drawn craft it quickly became apparent that, apart from fictional accounts such as *The Charities* in Roman mythology and the adventurer in Bishop Francis Godwin's pioneering book *The Man in the Moone*, there appeared to be precisely none. Indeed, the notion of a craft pulled by geese seems to me a wholly unrealistic one. How would the birds be trained, harnessed, steered, etc? If such a feat *were* possible surely Nelson would have had to be a specialist in this particular area, performing with his obedient geese on a regular basis rather than just this one occasion. I was, however, unable to locate record of any such act either at that time or since.

Something was beginning to bother me about the (admittedly limited) information I had managed to unearth about this bridge disaster; there never seemed to be any mention of the clown *after* the crossing's collapse. The reports that I had gave no indication as to whether Nelson was injured or involved in the rescue efforts; indeed, he had no place in the narrative at all save its introduction.

In Mrs. Bentall's firsthand account of the events of that day she states that "Someone shouted, 'Here he comes!' and the geese could just be seen coming around the bend of the river," but even she, who survived that day's events unharmed, never actually mentions seeing the clown. The article cited in the *Top Hat* piece gives a remarkably similar account: "As the clown approached the air rang with cries of 'Here come the geese!' but very few people noted that the bridge failed to retain its convex form."

I felt a creeping sense of dread as the possibility dawned upon me that Nelson the clown (or at the very least his washtub voyage) could, in fact, have been a work of mischievous fiction; a practical joke gone horribly awry.

Imagine a situation where an individual, perhaps even the clown himself, informs another about this upcoming amazing event: a man is to be pulled several miles up the river in a tub drawn by six white geese. Given that such a thing was and is, if not entirely impossible then at least wholly unprecedented, is it not reasonable to speculate that this individual may have been making a joke at the other's expense? If we then presume that the second individual, completely taken in by the other's falsehood, takes it upon his or her self to inform others around them, we are quickly faced with a situation where the story is spread throughout the whole town as an absolute truth. The community's collective excitement grows and arrangements are made to be at certain locations at certain times in order to obtain the best vantage point. The day and time of the event arrives and the people's enthusiasm reaches fever pitch in anticipation of seeing the hilarious spectacle. Suddenly, someone spots some geese rounding the river's bend in the distance and calls out "Here he comes!" Everyone rushes onto the bridge, clamoring to get a glimpse of the comedian, but the structure cannot bear their collective weight and collapses into the icy water.

The idea that the disaster might, in reality, have been caused by a hoax and that the true story of the bridge's collapse might actually be rather different to the accepted version of events was both thrilling

FUNERALS AT ST. NICHOLAS CHURCH, GREAT YARMOUTH.

and worrying to me. On the one hand I had the notion that I would really have achieved something if, during the course of my meagre investigations, I had uncovered a forgotten truth, long buried in the presumably folkloric retelling of the tragedy. However, if that were the case, might it not then be true that the facts had been hidden because of the town's embarrassment at the reality? Would we not then be left with a dark tale of the gullible folk of Great Yarmouth losing their children to the river all because of a cock and bull story? Better to blame someone, anyone, for the carnage surely? But, a clown? Yes, naturally a clown. What better way remember that it was idiocy that brought down the bridge that day? The truth would be encoded within the tale, hidden from those who do not know, but the central message would remain the same; beware the fool.

I had all but convinced myself at least. And so, with a mix of wonder and trepidation, I decided to seek out further information on the disaster, information that would either prove or disprove my theory. All I needed to do was find a single mention of Nelson the clown *after* the bridge's collapse and my hypothesis would at least require a slight rethink. I set to Googling around once more and, in time, managed to get in touch with John McBride, the current editor of *Yarmouth Archaeology*, a periodical published annually by the Great Yarmouth & District Archaeological Society since 1979. Mister McBride, in turn, was kind enough to put me in touch with some very helpful people down at the Yarmouth Central Library to whom I explained my situation in a short letter. Expectantly, I awaited a response.

• • •

It was mid July when a package filled with photocopied clippings and articles arrived through the post, courtesy of the generous archival staff down in Yarmouth. There were many interesting documents enclosed: details of the bridge's construction in 1829 penned by the then Mayor of Great Yarmouth, Robert Cory, the very man who commissioned its creation; articles about a picture depicting the bridge's collapse painted by local artist George Henry Harrison which sold for £1550 in 1999 and, of course, numerous pieces giving details of the collapse itself. I began picking through the photocopies, highlighting relevant passages and comparing the data in each with the information I already had. One undated clipping entitled "The Catastrophe At Great Yarmouth" appeared to have seen print only weeks after the disaster.

"The jury at Great Yarmouth have made but little progress in their important investigation during the past week … The total loss of life may now be correctly estimated at 78 … The residents of the place … describe the continual passing of bodies to the church, taken in connection with the melancholy event which was the cause of death, as one of the most distressing ever witnessed."

Another article taken from the *Yarmouth Mercury* in 1945 commemorates the centenary of the event by reprinting the very piece, which ran in the *Norwich Mercury* only six days after the collapse. This piece, like many of the others in the package, gives the name of Nelson's company as Cook(e)'s Circus. However, it also omits any mention of the clown in any portion of its text save the preamble. As I examined article after article the same story was repeated over and over again, right down to the cries of "Here come the geese!" which preceded the disaster. Nelson was nowhere to be found and, in my head, my theory was all but proven. That was, until I came across one small clipping.

Under the same "Yarmouth Porthole" heading, which I had already seen on several of the other photocopies (and therefore assumed to be a regular column in the *Yarmouth Mercury*), I read a piece entitled "More facts on bridge collapse." The article began in very similar fashion to those I had previously read, stating that the bridge had given way under the weight of 400 people who had gathered there that day to watch a clown sail down the river in a washtub pulled by geese. However, under the subheading "More facts," the piece went on to explain something that no other had even touched upon.

"Mr. H. T. G. Tinker, the Yarmouthian now domiciled in Norwich who is an authority on our theatres and the people who have performed in them, is researching and inquiring as diligently as ever.... It seems that Nelson was pulling a fast one that day. Not that he had any intention of causing any distress, but the act he performed had a premature and gloomy conclusion.... Dicky Usher, a noted clown in his day, is said to have developed this act as a publicity stunt. He was towed along the Thames from Westminster Bridge to Waterloo Bridge by geese.... It was copied by other clowns, Tom Batty, Nelson and Twist.... Although the geese were harnessed … the tub was really drawn by a small steam boat with a rope weighted so that it was underwater.... He sends me a copy of a playbill, or poster, for a Hartlepool tub-and-geese tow which, it was said, Nelson was presenting for the 191st time. After all this time it is sad to contemplate that there was a catch in it. If it had been known, the anger in Yarmouth would have been even greater. The recriminations were bitter enough as it was."

Excitedly, I Googled the name "Dicky Usher" and was rewarded with the following information from CircusHistory.org: "Richard 'Dicky' Usher was a native of Liverpool and a popular entertainer there at the Olympic Circus from as early as 1808. A trainer of geese and cats, he was the first clown to use the trick of being pulled down river in a tub by a pair of geese." And so, as easily as that, the truth of Nelson's washtub voyage was finally confirmed and my flight of fancy came to an end.

Credit: Leah Moore

I should like offer my sincerest apologies to all the people of Great Yarmouth whose integrity was brought into question during my wild hypothesizing; it was never my intention to cause any offense to any person or persons living or dead. On the other hand, you must admit that it made for a marvelous story; a spine chilling twist in an already tragic and macabre tale. Even now, it seems so eerily poignant to me that a clown should be the one to cause such a catastrophe; charming almost an entire generation of Great Yarmouth's sons and daughters to their deaths in a manner so spectacular it would surely inspire envy in even the fabled Pied Piper himself. The whole story reads like some gloomy fable whose bleak message seems only too clear: sometimes death comes disguised as a good time and the price is paid not only by those who embrace it but by all who surround them. An air of something peculiar and shuddersome lingers about the bridge collapse, a feeling that cold hard facts are powerless to dispel. As one (unnamed) contemporary commentator is reputed to have written, "Wisecrackers in the town had shaken their heads and prophesised disaster when it was announced that the benefit was to take place on a Friday.... A foolish man was to do a foolish trick, and foolish people rushed to see. Given the same conditions, the accident must have happened, no matter what the day, although doubtless it would be difficult to convince the superstitious of that fact."


**JOHN REPPION** was born in Liverpool, England in 1978. His writing career began in 2003 when he collaborated with his wife Leah Moore on a proposal for a six issue mini series entitled *Wild Girl*. The proposal was accepted and the series was published by Wildstorm in 2004/05. John's interests in fortean phenomena, esoterica, folklore, philosophy, theology and horror have led to his writing articles and reviews for numerous magazines and periodicals including *Fortean Times, Strange Attractor, The End Is Nigh* and *Revenant Magazine*. He continues to script comics in partnership with his wife and hopes to do so for many years to come.

# THE BLACK FLASH OF CAPE COD:
## TRUE HEIR OF SPRING-HEELED JACK
### By Theo Paijmans

"The Provincetown Phantom, better known as The Black Flash, is legend now, and his daring exploits, agility, strength and size grow greater and greater as the years go by."– Robert Ellis Cahill, "The Provincetown Phantom," *New England's Mad & Mysterious Men*, 1984

Cape Cod stretches out into the grey ocean like a crooked finger, forever beckoning westward, to the safety of the dry land. On its very tip lies the little community of Provincetown, a place of many marvels. Perhaps this is due to its unique geography, huddled so close to the vastness of the Atlantic Ocean. There is something to be said for this enchanted place, where sky, sea, and land meet in a precarious balance. Provincetown has a rich heritage. It is said that the Pilgrims touched land here in 1620, and wrote America's First Constitution. Those who dig deep enough into this past, find strange tales, fleeting rumors, and impossible anomalies that form an uncanny signature to the very spot. Thus Provincetown's hidden history numbers sea serpent sightings and haunted houses,[1] but nothing has been more disturbing and strange than the legend of the Black Flash.

In the late 1930s, a frightening and phantomlike creature plagued Provincetown with its presence and held its inhabitants in an ice-cold grip of fear. According to tradition, only recently established, The Black Flash had emerged from the dunes one October evening in 1938, "an elusive superman, a super-human leaping lizard, dressed in black – all in black…"[2] The visitations of the phantom were to last seven years. Then, in 1945, its activity stopped abruptly and the entity disappeared without a trace, never to be seen again. It was named The Black Flash of Provincetown, because of its seemingly supernatural agility, a fitting moniker for a black clad phantom, a dark denizen that might not have been of this world.

Until now, printed sources concerning this phantomlike creature, which by nature of his agility came to be seen as an entity of the Spring-Heeled Jack typology, have been of very recent date. The late Robert Ellis Cahill, a chronicler of the strange byways, ghostly lore, and curious tales of New England, rescued these strange events from oblivion by including a chapter on the Black Flash in his *New England's Mad & Mysterious Men*, which was published in 1984. This marks the beginning of the saga of The Black Flash in print.

From Cahill we learn that The Black Flash was described as "a giant monster," a phantomlike creature dressed in black, "black hood, black cape, black face but his fierce eyes and long pointed ears were a glowing silver." During a frightful evening encounter with a woman on Commercial Street near the Town Hall in the second week of November 1938, she described it as "black, all black, with eyes like balls of flame, and he was big, real big... maybe eight feet tall. He made a sound, a loud buzzing sound, like a June bug on a hot day, only louder... he disappeared like a flash."[3]

Other encounters and similar descriptions would follow. Writes Cahill: "Within the next three weeks, four other people had similar experiences in downtown Provincetown. The Black Flash either jumped out at them from behind a tree, or dropped down before them from a rooftop. Two of his victims were husky men, and although one man reported that he chased him, he said he was no match for the speed and agility of the Black Flash."[4]

Those who had had their luckless encounters with the elusive phantom agreed on its height, black cape, almost superhuman agility, and (sometimes) silver ears. In one instant, when it was cornered by the Provincetown police in a schoolyard surrounded by a ten foot fence, a flashlight shining on its face revealed "a mask, which looked like an old flour-screen without its handle, painted silver and strapped to the phantom's head."[5] The Black Flash then escaped over a fence. During another encounter one teenager alleged that the phantom had spit blue flames into his face. Then there is the farmer who allegedly emptied his rifle at The Black Flash, whereupon the phantom merely laughed and leaped over an eight-foot hedge.[6]

The Black Flash's final appearance was on "a cold December afternoon, with a thick fog rolling in from the sea." Some children, who were playing hide-and-seek, suddenly saw something on a hill that turned out to be the elusive fiend. The children ran back to the house with The Black Flash in pursuit. The unnerving encounter ended when one of the children threw a bucket of water over the phantom from the roof. After that, no more was heard of the Black Flash.[7]

There are rumors to this day that The Black Flash was, in fact, three or four Provincetown men who decided to play a prank on the community. This might explain why sometimes the phantom seemed to be at two places at once, or, as Cahill writes, "he'd be reported on one side of town, and a moment later, someone would call and say he was on the other side of town, two miles away."[8]

Cahill learned from Francis Marshall, who became Provincetown's Police Chief in 1959, that he knew who The Black Flash was but he refused to identify the culprit. "I will tell you this though... The Black Flash wasn't just one person. He was four men, who sometimes played the part alone, and sometimes together. Two are dead now, but the others have a hell of a time when they get together, reminiscing about the times they scared the hell out of their friends and neighbors in Provincetown."[9] When a reporter for the *Toronto Star* interviewed Marshall in 1988, he told him: "People wondered how the Flash could be in two places almost simultaneously, as some reports indicated. I believe it's because he was actually three men. Yes, I know who they were, but I'm not telling. They're all dead now, but they have relatives here."[10]

The legend of The Black Flash found its way into the *Toronto Star* article and other books.[11] Fortean researcher and author Mike Dash noted the apparent similarity between Provincetown's Black Flash and Spring-Heeled Jack: "So precisely does the Phantom's story mirror that of Spring-heeled Jack that it must be possible that the whole tale is a hoax based directly on the legend of the Victorian bogeyman," Dash comments.[12] He further remarks in a footnote: "A search of available local newspapers (mainly from the Boston area) for late 1938 by Michael Shoemaker has turned up no confirmation of this essentially oral Provincetown tradition."[13]

**Cabin fever stories start**

Since Shoemaker conducted his researches a number of newspapers have converted their archives into digital files that can be perused online. As a result I was able to find that Provincetown had its own newspaper at the time, the *Provincetown Advocate*, which was published from 1869 to 1970. Many issues of *The Advocate* – a four to six page weekly newspaper – have been digitized and are accessible online.[14] And there I found an actual, contemporary confirmation of the Black Flash of Provincetown; Robert Ellis Cahill had indeed reported on strange events that had actually stirred the Provincetown community in the late 1930s. It also confirmed that the name of the elusive creature was in use back then, right from the start. And on the basis of the accounts I found, which differ from the versions in use since Cahill, who was to be the primary source for all that has been written about The Black Flash since 1984, we can now draw some tentative conclusions about The Black Flash phenomenon.

On October 10, 1939 *The Advocate* published an article on its front page, headed "Fall Brings Out The "Black Flash." I quote the article verbatim:

> Joe Berger (Jeremiah Digges to you) says it's "Bowleg Bill," "the seagoing cowboy," back from a date with the Sea Witch of Goucester, Howard Slade ain't made up his mind but he knows it ain't Benny Regular. Ma Hunt said if a man grabbed her she would hold on. Chief Tony Tarvers said it's all a lot guerry, or something like it, and he's getting gol darned tired – or something like it – looking for the "Black Flash" and if he don't get some sleep nights he'll be thinking he's the "Black Flash."
>
> The winter may be long, the winter may be cold and we all may be eating Charlie Moller's sea gulls before the summer visitors begin to bud, but from the way it's starting it should be one of the best winters in recent Provincetown history.
>
> It ain't usually until 'cabin fever' time that the balmy

stories start. After folks have been penned up here for too long a time, in too little space, with just the same faces to look at every morning, afternoon, and evening, then the crazy yarns begin circulating.

But winter seems to be shutting in early this year. Here it is only October and the "Black Flash" has been prowling, scaring kids so that they won't go out nights and won't go to bed, grabbing women, jumping over ten foot hedges with no trouble at all. "Chair springs on his feet" is the explanation.

Newspapers over the country have taken up the story and the radio carries word of the daily exploits of Provincetown's "Black Flash."

Yet only one person, after intensive investigation, swears he saw the "Black Flash" and that was Capt. Phineus Blackstrap who met him out on Helltown Road late Monday night.

"I'm damned sartin I saw 'im," stated the Capt. under oath. "But that ain't nothing. We've had the 'Black Flash' here every fourth year since I was man and boy and he never harmed no one. Some usta say he was looking for his vessel that was lost [in] the Race and others usta say that he has a date to eat skully-joes with the Devil out at Peaked Hill when the first ones is ripe. I never seen him without he's gnawing away at a skully-jo."

"Sure he kin move fast, " added Capt. Blackstrap, "but he never does no one no harm. He's a native he won't even pass the time o'day with you."[15]

A week later, two allusions to the Black Flash appeared in *The Advocate*. One was made during a report of Provincetown's first community Halloween party, which was attended by some 600 children and adults: "Many of the youngsters came in costume and a hit of the evening was the 'Black Flash,' terror of Provincetown for the past weeks, who gave himself up and walked into the arms of the police. But instead of being booked for scaring people out of their wits, Chief Tarvers handed three-year-old Manuel Jason, Jr. a dollar for the best costume."[16]

The second was a very short announcement: "Next week I'll tell you all about Truro's "Black Flash,"[17] but this was never done. Instead, a week after that announcement, a short article was published, stating that "Chief of Police Anthony P. Tarvers this morning absolutely denied the rumors current that the so-called 'Black Flash' had been captured. 'As far as I am concerned the "Black Flash" is dead and gone,' said the Chief..."[18] Except for one reference to another anomalous event in the nearby town of Wellfleet, this heralded the end of the contemporary newspaper reporting of Provincetown's *Advocate*. In 1949, ten years later, *The Advocate* reprinted these two articles in a short retrospective without comment.[19]

## The Wellfleet Tarzan

Provincetown was not the only Cape Cod town to experience a series of anomalous events. Around the time that the Black Flash had ceased operating – or at least, newspaper coverage on the phantom had ceased – in the nearby town of Wellfleet, something was making the villagers equally uneasy. It was nicknamed "Tarzan," apparently because of the strange sounds it made.

> With Tarzan on the loose in the Paine Hollow section of South Wellfleet, the good neighbors there are shivering in their beds these nights – and quite cold it is, at that.
>
> "Tarzan," in case you don't know, is the name of our local phantom, a sequel to Provincetown's "Black Flash," maybe. Anyhow, the people were out the other night, armed with clubs and hammers and shot guns to track down the source of the strange noises that had tormented them for several days. They combed Paine Hollow with minute precision, but "Tarzan" remained elusive.

Some say that it was just a combination of a lot of things. Some say that Paul Piper's steer was misbehavin', cause Paul locked him up during deer week so that he wouldn't get nicked by short-sighted hunters. But do they know? Can they prove it?

The residents scoff at the thought of a phantom "Tarzan" swinging through the tree tops of South Wellfleet, yodelling like a sick sea-clam to scare little boys. But the good neighbors look beneath their beds before retiring these nights – I betcha![20]

### Preliminary conclusions

Though these newspaper articles on the subject are few in number, when juxtaposed with Cahill's account, an alternative picture of the events emerges. According to *The Advocate*, the reign of terror did not begin in 1938 but in 1939, and it did not last till 1945, but a mere couple of weeks, proof of which can be found in the fact that 10 years later *The Advocate* reprinted these articles without adding any new details. But the claim in *The Advocate* that newspapers across the U.S.A. had written about the exploits of the Black Flash, I cannot, at this time, substantiate. While I have exhausted a great many digital newspaper archives and found nothing pertaining to the elusive phantom, the possibility remains that newspapers on a local, instead of regional, level might have devoted some space to Provincetown's Black Flash. As to the alleged radio airings that the first article on The Black Flash in *The Advocate* referred to, the verdict remains open. If not a case of typical editorial hyperbole, it might on one level explain the relative scarcity of articles on the exploits of The Black Flash, which were quite numerous if we are to take Cahill's account literally.[21]

As to the tantalizing announcement in *The Advocate* that all was going to be told about The Black Flash, but instead a short comment was published by Chief of Police Tarvers that The Black Flash was dead and gone, this might indeed indicate that in a little community such as Provincetown with only 4,500 inhabitants, Tarvers become aware of the identity of The Black Flash, and in a subsequent communication with *The Advocate*, had decided to let the matter rest as he had made sure, perhaps through a stern warning or a severe reprimand to those involved, that the reign of The Black Flash had ended. Or perhaps the persons behind the prank – if that it was – had relayed their activities to Wellfleet.

All in all, what essentially may be relegated to the realm of oral embellishment or folklore are the exploits of The Black Flash as recounted by Cahill, who had as his sources Al Janard from Provincetown and Francis Marshall. At least, until perhaps one day someone is incredibly lucky to find hidden in an attic somewhere in Provincetown a diary, say, or a moth eaten costume, we have no other contemporary documentation than those few articles in *The Advocate*. None of the encounters or spectacular incidents as listed by Cahill are found in the pages of *The Advocate*.

So who was Robert Ellis Cahill? Author of more than 40 books on New England's ghosts, witches, and pirates, a scuba diver in his early days, Cahill had long been interested in New England history, pirates, and sunken treasures. "I had done all this research...I just kept building files up and I did some freelance writing. So I said, 'Now that I'm retired I'll write these books for fun.' It was just a whim and it grew and grew." Cahill founded the Salem Witch's Dungeon Museum, which opened in the 1970s, and the New England Pirate Museum, which opened in Salem in 1994. His wife Sandra Howard Cahill, who survived him when he died of heart failure in 2005, lovingly described him as "a storyteller. I heard all of his stories about 100 times, but they were always interesting..."[22] And Vermont author and folklorist Joseph Citro writes appreciatively about Cahill that "just about everywhere I went looking for ghosts and goblins, I always seemed to find myself following Mr. Cahill's footprints."[23] Cahill's background in law enforcement and solid reputation might perhaps explain why former Provincetown Police Chief Francis Marshall told him the things he knew.

### Heir of Spring-Heeled Jack

But what then, about the often-made connection with that other elusive fiend, that prototype of agility, almost supernatural swiftness, and bizarre strangeness, Spring-Heeled Jack? As Mike Dash has demonstrated in his groundbreaking essay on Spring-Heeled Jack, the legend has given rise to numerous misinterpretations and misconceptions. The current popular perception of Spring-Heeled Jack as a black clad, flames belching, and almost alien apparition was actually based on one encounter in 1838, with Jane Alsop:

> At about a quarter to nine o'clock... she heard a violent ringing at the gate at the front of the house, and on going to the door to see what was the matter, she saw a man standing outside, of whom she enquired what was the matter, and requested he would not ring so loud. The person instantly replied that he was a policeman, and said "For God's sake, bring me a light, for we have caught Spring-heeled Jack here in the lane." She returned into the house and brought a candle, and handed it to the person, who appeared enveloped in a long cloak, and whom she at first really believed to be a policeman. The instant she had done so, however, he threw off his outer garment, and applying the lighted candle to his breast, presented a most hideous and frightful appearance, and vomited forth a quantity of blue and white flames from his mouth, and his eyes resembled red balls of fire. From the hasty glance, which her fright enabled her to get of his person, she observed that he wore a large helmet, and his dress, which appeared to fit him very tight, seemed to her to resemble white oil skin. Without uttering a sentence, he darted at her, and catching her partly by her dress and the back part of her neck, placed her head under one of his arms, and commenced tearing her gown with his claws, which she was certain were of some metallic substance. She screamed out as loud as she could for assistance, and by considerable exertion got away from him, and ran towards the house to get in. Her assailant, however, followed her, and caught her on the steps leading to the half-door, when he again used considerable

violence, tore her neck and arms with his claws, as well as a quantity of hair from her head; but she was at length rescued from his grasp by one of her sisters. Miss Alsop added, that she had suffered considerably all night from the shock she had sustained, and was then in extreme pain, both from the injury done to her arm, and the wounds and scratches inflicted by the miscreant about her shoulders and neck with his claws or hands."[24]

But Spring-Heeled Jack emerged from an almost protoplasmic cauldron in which the elements still had to settle and with their origin dating as far back as 1803 and stretching forward in time until this very day – if we are to put credence in the accounts that float around the internet on various forums devoted to anomalies and the supernatural. Writes Dash: "Unique though he has always seemed to be in the ufological and Fortean literature, Jack is, in fact, merely the best known of a host of more or less similar figures who have appeared in various locations between 1803 and the present day. Taken together, these supplementary cases suggest that the ideas of a devil on earth and of a spring-heeled man are deeply rooted in a number of different cultures."[25]

Spring-Heeled Jack over the years was described as having various forms, shapes, and appearances. His most telling attributes, that of the ability to jump or leap over greater distances and heights than normal man was capable of and the fire belching, still had to win firm ground. What gave rise to this almost unanimous and quite erroneous perception of Spring-Heeled Jack was the highly influential but also highly imaginative article by J. Vyner in the English UFO publication *Flying Saucer Review* that was published in 1961.[26] Vyner also attempted to establish some antecedents suggesting that the Spring-Heeled Jack phenomenon had spread to the United States. And since Cahill's chapter on The Black Flash, others have classed him, or it, in the same category, which seems fair, as the earliest newspaper account on The Black Flash refers to his ability to jump over ten foot hedges and "chair springs on his feet." Vyner – and to my knowledge it is the first time that such a list on Spring-Heeled

Jack sightings in the United States was compiled – does not refer to The Black Flash, which on one hand serves to demonstrate just how little known The Black Flash was in 1961. Vyner does mention sightings in Louisville, Kentucky in 1880, ties in the non-related Mad Gasser of Mattoon, and the sightings of "birdmen" in Chehalis in 1948 and Houston, Texas in 1953. Vyner's list has proven to be most influential, with other Fortean researchers usually embroidering on this list, mostly by adding to it more "flying men" sightings of dubious provenance.[27]

Like Dash, I am dismissive of Vyner's list. A closer examination of these events shows that it consists of incidents that involved the sightings of allegedly flying men or entities, none of them jumping, leaping or otherwise engaged in the typical, by now folkloristic, aspects of Spring-Heeled Jack behavior. Vyner justifies his choice of Fortean events by speculating that Spring-Heeled Jack was an entity in need of wings:

> The enigma of Springheel Jack's astounding leaps is, like the siren's song, not entirely beyond conjecture. It is possible that a being from a highgravity planet might be able to duplicate some of his feats... All accounts of Jack's feats seem to indicate that he had perfect control over his mighty bounds... I am inclined to think the solution must lie in the possession of a device for neutralising gravity. Normally, the user would reduce his weight to a point at which he could walk normally while retaining the capacity for tremendous leaps. Increasing the power would enable him to soar, or even float. But he would then lose control... unless he had wings, serving as control surfaces... Springheel Jack in his former incarnation as Icarus. No fixed abode.[28]

Dash has demonstrated that Vyner's article was based on considerable misconception, and Vyner's speculation, inviting as it may be, stems from that very misconception. Moreover, since Vyner's motif for including what are basically anomalous sightings of flying entities has been proven to be incorrect – and in at least one instance, that of the often quoted Chehalis incident, I found additional materials that warrant serious doubts as to the nature of the sighting – it is best to discard this list altogether.[29] For instance, while the 1948 Chehalis incident is still riding the waves in Fortean literature as a true, unexplained anomaly, its very refutation by the family of the eyewitness in 1976 is never mentioned, so we publish it here for the first time.

The Chehalis sighting, made by Mrs. Bernice Zaikowski in January 1948, received widespread coverage in American newspapers.

> Such coverage, however, did not exactly delight the Zaikowski family. "They (the newspapers) made it so dumb," explained Mrs. George Zaikowski this week. "She (Bernize) was old country and when she tried to explain what she saw it sounded weird, hard to understand." Particularly irksome was the fact that, while both metropolitan dailies played up the event, they did not give equal space to the explanation. The Zaikowskis learned later that the apparition was a man in a "parakite," forerunner to the present day hang glider. "It was about the time they were trying to find someplace to use hang gliders," Mrs. George Zaikowski recalls. "There were those who felt this area would have been a good place for it." To Mrs. Bernize Zaikowski, though, born in Poland and used to the old country ways, the contraption was something strange.[30]

Therefore, an update is severely needed on the cases that usually serve to demonstrate that the Spring-Heeled Jack phenomenon visited the United States, and with that in mind I have compiled a new list. (See addendum.)

But how, if The Black Flash was one, three or four men, did he manage to jump over tall hedges and display his agility that outclassed even the burliest of men? Are such feats even humanly possible? These questions are crucial as they lift The Black Flash from the realm of the supernatural and the truly anomalous into what we could classify as natural, albeit bizarre, occurrences. All in all, if The Black Flash consisted of a group of men of flesh and blood, I suggest that this group could have very well been involved not in the construction of springs under their boots – I have yet to see boots with springs enabling one to jump to great heights and to land safely without breaking ones ankles – but in the exercise of an unusual form of sports. For an example of this, we have to turn to the 21st century suburbs of Paris, France, where a street sport known as free running originated and is currently being practiced by certain factions of youth culture throughout Europe. Free running, also known as Parkours or *l'art du déplacment* (the art of displacement), has as its aim to conquer obstacles in the most fluid and fastest way possible, using the principal abilities of the human body. The obstacles can be anything in a typical urban environment: branches, concrete walls, railings, etc. Free running or Parkours itself is derived from Georges Hébert (1875-1957), a pioneering French physical education instructor. Hébert's system, the idea for which came to him as early as 1902 and then developed while he at sea, was called *Methode Naturelle* (Natural Method). Practitioners would exercise their craft through walking, running, jumping, climbing, balancing, throwing, lifting, and swimming. Hébert also authored a number of books on the subject.[31]

While I would not suggest that Provincetown knew four or three secret practitioners of Hébert's *Methode Naturelle*, anyone who has seen a free running group in action these days is amazed at their agility in overcoming and scaling walls, balustrades, hedges, and other obstacles with grace, prowess, and ease. If The Black Flash consisted of a small group of bored – or perhaps inspired – Provincetown men, perhaps they formed their own natural method and thus were able to engage in feats such as jumping over hedges, feats that must have seemed astounding to unsuspecting bystanders in 1939. And in time, as Cahill states, these feats were embellished to truly folkloric degrees.

Was The Black Flash then a bizarre phenomenon of human, instead of supernatural, nature? All the evidence we have at our disposal strongly points in that direction. Not only did rumors float around from the start that the identity or identities behind Provincetown's black phantom were known (and we note the parallel with the legend of Spring-Heeled Jack), but when we take endeavors like Free Running and Hébert's *Methode Naturelle* into account, combined with the way impressive events are embellished over the years by each generation, the theory that The Black Flash was a human agent instead of a supernatural, or truly anomalous, one still holds.[32] However, as we do not have any definitive evidence that this was indeed the case, in all fairness and as all good Forteans should, we leave the door ajar for any other explanation.

What remains is the enigma of The Black Flash, who may be America's true contender to Spring-Heeled Jack, and in lesser fashion, that overlooked anomaly of the Wellfleet, Tarzan, which might have had the same origin as Provincetown's black-clad phantom. Whether The Black Flash was a prank by a party of bored or, on the contrary, illuminated Provincetown men, or whether it was something more, not only was the Black Flash fitted with all the legendary attributes of London's infamous fiend, in time, he has become his own legend as well.

**Notes**

1. A few samples of Provincetown anomalies follow: Captain Jonas Hathaway and his two sailors, Peleg Howland and Joshua Delano, were brought to land in Boston by the fishing boat Mary Anne. They had had a terrible encounter with a strange and unknown sea monster, some distance from Provincetown's shore, from which they barely escaped with their lives. Two of them had sustained severe injuries, their boat crushed by the creature. They were unable to describe the creature in any detail, except "that it was not a sea serpent at all, but more of the reptile form, with a distinct body and great fins and a powerful tail. Its massive head, poised on a long, scaly neck, was inexpressibly ugly. In color it was singular dark reddish green with white underneath. It had projecting fangs and bulging eyes. ("A Sea Monster Attacks a Boat and Nearly Kills a Man," *Newark Daily Advocate*, Newark, Ohio, 1900-05-25.)

   There were rumors of ghosts, too, in old Provincetown. In 1935 a group of amateur psychics investigated a haunted house known to the community as Provincetown's "Ghost House." Its owner at the time, Mrs. Ralph Harlow, had complained that "spirits have played pranks for the past five years" in the 150-year-old house. "The séance began at 10:30 P.M. Until midnight, nothing happened. Then, as the nearby town hall clock chimed 12, the group was startled by the crashing of glass in an upstairs room. Mrs. Harlow and her guests raced upstairs and found the dish which for years had rested on a table, in fragments on the floor." ("Broken Glass Dish Is Only Mystery In Spook Search," *The Modesto Bee And News-Herald*, Modesto, California,1935-07-13.)

In January 1939, the thirty-foot long remains of an unknown creature washed ashore at Cape Cod, near the Wood End coast guard station. It had, according to one newspaper, 71 sections, complete with vertebrae, leg joints and a toothless skull, with the tail missing, and "...midway in the trunk, bones of what might have been frog-like feet protrude. In the center of the skull is a round hole. Old-timers believed the skeleton that of the famous Provincetown 'sea serpent' of 1886. Addison Ormsby, commander of the Wood End coast guard station, would not subscribe to this theory, but said: 'we have never seen anything like it before. I don't think it could be a whale or a black fish.'" ("Sea Serpent? 30-Foot Skeleton Washed to Shore in Massachusetts," *Mansfield News Journal*, Mansfield, Ohio, 1939-01-17.) It was later identified as the remains of a basking shark. "Prof. W.C. Schroeder, curator of fish at the Harvard Zoological Museum stated that 'it was nothing unusual.'" ("Saving The Sea Serpent," *San Antonio Express*, San Antonio, Texas, 1939-02-17.)

I have cited these newspapers more or less at random from my collection of 42 newspaper clippings of the event; the discovery was widely covered in newspapers throughout the United States and Canada, often accompanied by photographs of the coast guards and the remains of the creature and all agree on its features, although the length given differs from between 20 to 30 feet, and in one case 40 feet.

2. Robert Ellis Cahill, "The Provincetown Phantom," *New England's Mad & Mysterious Men*, Chandler-Smith Publishing House, Collectible Classics Series Number 4, 1984, pages 23.
3. Ibid. pages 23-24.
4. Ibid. Page 24.
5. Ibid. Page 28.
6. Ibid. Page 24.
7. Ibid. Pages 28-29.

8.  Ibid. Page 28.
9.  Ibid. Page 29.
10. Mitchell Smyth, Halloween Flashback: "How 'phantom' Joker terrorized a town," *Toronto Star*, 1988-10-29. Smith additionally interviewed an eyewitness of the capers of The Black Flash.
11. Joseph Citro, *Passing Strange: True Tales Of New England Hauntings and Horrors*, Houghton Mifflin, 1997, see the chapter "When the Devil came to Provincetown," pages 171-176. Citro acknowledges Cahill as his source. Jerome Clark, *Unexplained: Strange Sightings, Incredible Occurrences, and Puzzling Physical Phenomena*, Visible Ink Press, 1993, "Springheel Jack," pages 357-359, 2nd. Edition 1999, "Springheel Jack," pages 500-507. Follows Cahill through Dash. Also in Jerome Clark, *The UFO Encyclopedia*, Vol.2, 2nd edition, Omnigraphics, 1988, page 880. Cites Dash as source.
12. See <www.mikedash.com/investigations_jack_paper_2.htm>. Also in Mike Dash, "Spring-Heeled Jack: To Victorian Bugaboo from Suburban Ghost," *Fortean Studies*, vol. 3, edited by Steve Moore, pages 111-112. The internet version is preferred as it is an updated version of the print publication with many new details. Citro also made this connection.
13. See <www.mikedash.com/investigations_jack_paper_2.htm>.
14. See <ptownlib.com/Advocate%20Live.htm>.
15. "Fall Brings Out The 'Black Flash,' Hard Winter Certain As 'Cabin Fever' Stories Start," *The Advocate*, Provincetown, Massachusetts, 1939-10-26. Some explanation is needed here. Joe Berger was a Provincetown writer of some renown who wrote "Bowleg Bill" and used as his pen name "Jeremiah Digges." See: "Joe Berger Turns To Books For Boys. Third In Series Of 'Jim' Stories Will Appear Next Month," *The Advocate*, Provincetown, Massachusetts, 1946-07-25. Berger also wrote the *Cape Cod Pilot*, which was published in 1937 by the Modern Pilgrim Press, Provincetown. This was a work underwritten by the Federal Writers Project, Works Project Administration for the State of Massachusetts. Helltown was the nickname for Provincetown.
16. "Youngsters Enjoy Hallowe'en Event. Police Head Reports Usual Mischief Missing This Year," *The Advocate*, Provincetown, Massachusetts, 1939-11-02.
17. H. Hughes Snow, Jr., "Truro Tells," *The Advocate*, Provincetown, Massachusetts, 1939-11-02.
18. "Chief Denies Current Rumors," *The Advocate*, Provincetown, Massachusetts, 1939-11-09.

19. "The Advocate Was Saying. Ten Years Ago. October 26, 1939. Fall Brings Out The 'Black Flash,'" *The Advocate*, Provincetown, Massachusetts, 1949-10-27. "Chief Denies Current Rumors," *The Advocate*, Provincetown, Massachusetts, 1949-11-10.

20. Fred Moran, "Tarzan Is Making Wellfleet Uneasy. Perhaps Only A Steer – Other Happenings In The Town," *The Advocate*, Provincetown, Massachusetts, 1939-12-14.

21. Radio reports on The Black Flash are quite possible. In 1932, for instance, Lowell Thomas aired over a coast-to-coast radio hook-up from New York details of the Snallygaster, the "weird monster of Middletown Valley." "Mr. Thomas devoted about five or six minutes of his 15 minutes news summary to a description of the antics of the strange creature, which was the talk of the county just a week or so ago. Thousands of radio listeners from Boston to Seattle heard how the 'snallygaster' supposedly first swooped into Middletown Valley, frightening several reputable citizens nearly out of their wits. Mr. Thomas quoted from the story of the monster as it appeared in *The Frederick News* and referred to other newspapers which carried the unique tale..." From "'Snallygaster' Story Goes On Air Monday. Lowell Thomas Tells About It In The News," *The News*, Frederick, Maryland, 1932-12-13. In 1930, a fictional radio show called *The Shadow*, a fictional mystery detective from pulp magazine publisher Street and Smith with "the power to cloud men's minds so that they cannot see him" was aired. The series lasted 21 episodes until 1954. One actor named Orson Welles featured in the fourth radio show in 1937. See <www.shadowsanctum.net/radio/radio.html>. On October 30, 1938, Orson Welles aired his famous adaptation of H.G. Wells' *The War Of The Worlds*. Coincidentally, this was the date that The Black Flash, according to Cahill, came shambling from the Provincetown sand dunes.

22. Tom Long, "Robert Cahill, 70; was county sheriff, chronicler of Salem," *The Boston Globe*, 2005-06-23.

23. Joseph Citro, *Passing Strange: True Tales Of New England Hauntings and Horrors*, Houghton Mifflin, 1997, page 315.

24. *"Outrage On A Young Lady," The Times*, 1838-02-22. See also: Mike Dash, "Spring-Heeled Jack: To Victorian Bugaboo from Suburban Ghost," *Fortean Studies*, vol. 3, edited by Steve Moore, pages 52-53, or <www.mikedash.com/investigations_jack_paper.htm>.

25. Mike Dash, "Spring-Heeled Jack: To Victorian Bugaboo from Suburban Ghost," *Fortean Studies*, vol. 3, edited by Steve Moore, pages 21-22.

Also <www.mikedash.com/investigations_jack_paper_2.htm>.

26. J. Vyner, "The Mystery Of Springheel Jack," *Flying Saucer Review*, May-June 1961, Vol. 7 No. 3, pages 3-6.

27. See for instance W. Ritchie Benedict, "Spring-Heeled Jack Does America," *Fate*, June 2005, pages 18-26. In his article, Benedict lists a case of a strange entity seen in Mexico, Missouri, that he located in the *Daily Sun*, New Brunswick, 1883-12-14. The entity was described as "a lean monster man, eight and ten feet in height, wearing a long cloak, and going about with his head bowed in an abstracted way, but occasionally glaring at those it meets with small, glittering eyes said to resemble those of a cat or some wild beast." Benedict notes a fascinating resemblance with an entity report three years earlier, published in the December issue of the *Victoria Daily Colonist* and recounted by John Robert Colombo in his 1994 book *Strange Stories*. Benedict wrote to the University of Missouri for additional data concerning the Mexico, Missouri incident, but the answer was that their holdings of newspapers didn't go back that far. Benedict wonders, as the *Daily Sun* article cites the *Boston Globe* as its source, if additional details might be found there. I have located the *Boston Globe* article, which was published on December 12, but the wording is exactly the same. Jim Brandon, in his *Weird America*, Dutton, 1978, lists on page 92 a Spring-Heeled Jack-like entity, tall, thin, with a long nose and pointed fingers that terrorized Louisville on July 28, 1880: "He wore a sort of uniform, made of shiny fabric, and with a long cape and metallic helmet. On his chest under the cape was a large, bright light. His big thing seemed to be scaring people – particularly women – sometimes getting so familiar as to pull their clothing off. His favorite method of escape was by springing smoothly over high objects like haystacks or wagons, then vanishing on the other side." I have not been able to find the original account or any contemporary reference thereof; Brandon gives no source; it is doubtful that this account exists at all as a contemporary record.

28. J. Vyner, "The Mystery Of Springheel Jack," *Flying Saucer Review*, May-June 1961, Vol. 7 No. 3, Pages 5-6.

29. See for Dash's arguments in doing so: <www.mikedash.com/investigations_jack_paper_4.htm> or Mike Dash, "Spring-Heeled Jack: To Victorian Bugaboo from Suburban Ghost," *Fortean Studies*, vol. 3, edited by Steve Moore, pages 35-36.

30. Chuck Wilfong, "Beware! The Mothman Cometh," *The Daily Chronicle*, Washington, 1976-10-30.

31. See <en.wikipedia.org/wiki/Georges_H%C3%A9bert>.
32. Obviously unrelated, yet in good Fortean tradition, I'd like to mention to note that Joe Berger, who featured so heavily in the first Black Flash article, "sustained painful injuries when he fell and fractured his shoulder," while spending the winter in New Orleans. From: "Joe Berger Injured," *The Advocate*, Provincetown, Massachusetts, 1940-04-04.


## Addendum

I propose a new preliminary list, consisting of alleged events, sightings, and encounters with entities in America that feature one or more attributes of the Spring-Heeled Jack typology, which I compiled during my searches in various digital newspaper archives. The list is by no means all encompassing nor conclusive. Joseph Citro, for instance, refers to the Newhallville Ghost in his *Passing Strange* that would certainly make this list. I expect that, as more and more newspapers digitize their old issues, new cases will emerge.

As to the truthfulness of the accounts listed below, who can tell? Nineteenth century American newspapers had a distinct way of presenting outright yarns, tall tales, and hoaxes, as it was not considered unethical or beneath the standards of journalism. In some cases one almost feels a subtle sense of humor that would, of course, have been very much appreciated by a 19th century reader of these accounts; that very subtlety, which to us, now, is being lost. So we are left to ponder: Did those residents in Alma really see a beautiful lady in lingerie or an elephant with fire sprouting from its trunk? Was that Jesup farmer truly attacked by a headless ghost with a giant club that was able to jump 15 feet in the air or did that farmer exist at all? What matters more then is not so much the veracity of these claims and statements, but rather the way these ghosts, spirits, and hauntings were given certain attributes, such as leaping to great heights, emitting fire, and otherwise engaging in acts not unlike those of Spring-Heeled Jack. As any researcher involved in this kind of research realizes, the distinct typology of ghosts, entities, spirits, specters, and apparitions and their possible typological or folkloristic overlaps with UFO occupants, cryptozoological marvels, and biological impossibilities is difficult to sort out. A daunting task indeed, as I find more and more forgotten flaps, reports, and events in old, long since defunct newspapers that nevertheless excited, amazed, and sometimes frightened whole neighborhoods, towns, and generations and in those days, were the topic of the day.

*A preliminary list of entities, apparitions, specters, and ghosts in the United States that feature one or more attributes ascribed to Spring-Heeled Jack, 1885-1927:*

### 1885: The Lawrence Church steeple dancing ghost

In December, 1885, the people of Lawrence, "an aristocratic quarter of recent creation near Far Rockaway," were mystified and puzzled by "the appearance of a specter in the belfry of the Methodist Episcopal Church." Men gathered in dark places every night to observe the strange sight. "It flits about the belfry in the most nimble fashion, one time ascending to the apex of the steeple and at another executing a dance on the slanting roof. It plays hide and seek in the lattice work of the bell room, enlarging and decreasing in size according to the angle of observation. A remarkable thing is that it never appears on a Sunday night. The story of the strange sight has reached several villages, and every night scores of persons walk or drive to the vicinity of the Lawrence Church to verify it. Some of these declare that the specter has followed them home and hung around their residences for hours...Last Saturday night the strange figure was more than usually active, and scores of persons kept their eyes fixed on it until, benumbed by the cold, they were driven home. Half the village declares that at precisely ten o'clock the bell was tolled... Immediately after the tolling, three hearty amens were heard, and then the specter flattened itself out on the roof.... After a few minutes there was seen the liveliest skipping in and out of the lattice work, and then the phantom ran up and down the surface of the steeple, concluding by perching on the top, and disappearing in the direction of the grave yard..."

Source: "A Lively Ghost. Which is Causing Consternation Near far Rockaway. An Apparition which Haunts a Church Steeple and which is Supposed to Make its Appearance from a Graveyard," *Brooklyn Daily Eagle,*

Brooklyn, New York, 1885-12-07.

### 1885: The Long Island fire spitting ghost

"...After a rest of five years, a specter with a tongue of fire
has reappeared on the old Centerville race course, just south of
Woodhaven, and men and women congregate every night to witness
the strange sight. His ghostship appears promptly at a quarter to ten
o'clock and departs at twelve minutes after eleven... There is a dispute
whether the ghost wears a robe of white or a garment more the color
of sheep's wool. But on one other point there is no disagreement
– the ghost spits fire like a foundry chimney and leaves a sulphurous
odor behind it... It moves along space like a feather in the wind,
going a zigzag course. At regular intervals it spits fire. Scores of
persons have followed in its wake without getting close enough for
personal contact, and all declare that when the ghost comes to stop,
it invariably says 'Whoa!'"

Source: "A Fiery Tongue. The Latest Long Island Ghost Story. Supposed
to be the Phantom of a Murderer – A Disturbed Spirit which Spits Fire Like
a Foundry and Leaves a Wake of Sulphur Behind it," *Brooklyn Daily Eagle*,
Brooklyn, New York, 1885-12-18.

### 1889: The Wading River graveyard ghost with fire from its eyes

"They have a lively ghost at Wading River. Unlike the Blissville
spook that cried 'To wo! To who!' this Wading River specter keeps
perfect silence and strikes terror to the beholders by darting fire at
them out of its eyes... the figure's dress is smoky in color instead of
pure white. At 11:55 o'clock P.M. the ghost appears in the churchyard
and jumps around in the liveliest possible way, apparently trying to
read the inscriptions on the tombstones and locate itself properly. At
precisely 12 o'clock, M. the figure mounts to the top of a stone, lets go
twelve fiery darts and disappears from view entirely. It rarely appears
or disappears at the same point twice and the startled people do not
know where to look for it, but they have no difficulty in locating it
when the moments for the earth to open up and reveal the messenger
from sheol arrives... They say that long before the fiery object took
to practicing athletics in the graveyard it could be discerned playing
hide and seek in the church belfry, and on one occasion the bell was

rung violently at midnight..."

Source: "Down On Long Island. Wading River's Graveyard Inhabited by a Ghost. The Specter is Visible for Five Minutes and Fire Darts from Its Eyes," *Brooklyn Daily Eagle*, Brooklyn, New York, 1889-07-21.

## 1892: The Raymond Street fire spitting ghost

"The good people living on Raymond Street in the vicinity of the jail are greatly excited over the reported visitation of an inhabitant of the other world that has been seen in and around the jail... A colored youth standing hard by was observed to remark, while his eyes danced with excitement: '...it wuz a great big thing, seven or eleven feet high, all dressed in white, with horns on its head.'...A business man in the immediate vicinity... said: '...Those who have seen it probably imagined it... I have heard it described as being anywhere from seven to twelve feet high, dressed in white; some say with fire shooting out of its mouth...'"

Source: "Raymond Street Ghosts. A Coloured Youth 'Dun Seed One Wid His Own Eyes,'" *Brooklyn Daily Eagle*, Brooklyn, New York, 1892-12-25.

## 1897: the Auburn, New York, leaping ghost with a lantern

"Auburn, N.Y., Aug. 5 – Hundreds of people have been greatly annoyed by the antics of a new kind of ghost. It is in the habit of appearing at 1 o'clock at night, and is tall, clothed in white and carries a lantern. It does not glide, as most specters do, but bounds like a kangaroo.

"...rising from the center of the oat field a strange apparition, it was apparently the figure of a man clothed entirely in white. The ghostly figure stalked across the oat field, swinging a lantern in its hand. It advanced to the fence facing the round, and after flourishing his lantern up and down several times like a brakeman signalling a railroad train, the white figure gave a tremendous bound into the air and vanished from sight....About 10 o'clock the ghost appeared, carrying his lantern with him. The spectre made its appearance, apparently rising from the ground at the foot of a beech tree which stands at the west end of the field. The white robed figure dodged in and out, seen at one minute, the next lost to sight. After continuing his performance for a few minutes, the figure advanced boldly toward the astounded spectators. It came on with abounding movement, similar to that made by a kangaroo while in motion. When within a few feet of the spectators, the ghost stood motionless for a second, and after waving the lantern in the air three or four times, suddenly vanished from sight..."

Sources: "Novel Ghost. It Bounds Like a Kangaroo Instead of Gliding," *The Fort Wayne News*, Fort Wayne, Indiana, 1897-08-05. "An Uneasy Spirit. Stalks in an Auburn Oat Field. Draws Crowds To The Scene. All Attempts to Capture the Spectre Unsuccesful. Mysterious Figure Swings a Lantern Like a Brakeman and Boldly Confronts Spectators. But Vanishes If Approached," *The Sunday Herald,* Syracuse, New York, 1897-08-01.

### 1897: The Geigertown, Illinois black ghost

"That section of North Peoria, Il., known as Geigertown, is excited over the appearance of a strange black object that wanders around at night, chasing those who happen to be wandering along any of the dark and unfrequented streets and lanes of the village... many people claim that they have seen the black-robed figure parading the dark streets and alleys, and they say that if alone it always follows them..."

Source: "Black Ghost At Peoria. One Section of Town Frequented by an Off-Colored Spirit," *Dubuque Daily Herald*, Dubuque, Iowa, 1897-08-12.

### 1897: The Piermont, New York, swift and giant invulnerable ghost

"Some time ago the little village of Piermont, about four miles south of Nyack, N.Y., was intensely excited over the reputed appearance of a ghost... The ghost was described as fully eight feet tall, as pale as the driven snow, and as noiseless in its movements as death... Several attempts were made to capture it, but without success, and numerous revolver and rifle shots were fired at it without having the slightest effect. A sober, staid and reliable resident of Piermont said to a reporter of *The New York Times*: 'The people of the outside world may think we are acting like a lot of fools, but there is something very mysterious in the whole matter...If it is some man trying to play a joke on the people he must have an iron-clad hide and the wings of the wind, for pistol shots do not affect him and no one can get near him.'"

Source: "A Ghost Not Afraid of Bullets," *The McKean Democrat*, Smethport, Pennsylvania, 1897-11-05.

## 1899: The Hillsboro, Indiana headless leaping ghost

"Near Hillsboro, in western Indiana, there is a strip of wild, hilly country known as Red Hills, which for several years, according to the stories of reputable and reliable people, has been haunted by a headless ghost. Quite recently two farmers, driving through the hills after nightfall, were attacked by the ghost, which jumped into their wagon. Both deserted their team and fled in wild dismay. More recently a gang of coon hunters were stampeded, and none of them can be again persuaded to venture in that locality after night. Other people profess to have seen the same apparition, which came bounding toward them, frequently leaping 10 and 15 feet into the air, but disappearing when close at hand. Recently, says the *Cincinnati Enquirer*, William Pithoud, a farmer, makes declaration that as he was driving homeward the ghost appeared, armed with a huge club, and began belaboring his horses. Pithoud jumped out and fled in terror, never stopping until he reached the home of Harry Barton, who armed himself with a rifle and furnished Pithoud with a weapon. Together they returned to the scene of action, and they found the horses lying in a ditch, quivering with terror and showing every indication of having had a rough time."

Source: "Headless Ghost. An apparition That Wields a Big Club in Indiana," *Morning Times*, Cripple Creek, Colorado, 1899-12-20.

## 1908: The Alma, Colorado fire spitting elephant ghost

"Alma had a sensation this week in the shape of a ghost, which appeared at night. People coming from the saloons about midnight saw a strange sight, or imagined they did. One night the phantom was seen near the Thomas saloon, another time it was at the bridge, on Main Street. The courageous Almaites gave chase, but when they arrived at the spot the apparition had mysteriously disappeared. Some describe it as a beautiful woman, clad in the finest white lingerie. The spot where the beauty disappeared was fragrant with the perfume of roses and violets. Others again say it looked to them like a huge elephant, with streams of fire issuing from its trunk, and when they arrived at the spot where it had vanished, the smell of sulphur and brimstone permeated the air. The young ladies of Alma are frightened and will not venture forth in the evening without an escort. The gallant young men act with the greatest of pleasure in this capacity. So far, the 'spook' has not been caught, but if this should be the case, would summarily be dealt with."

Source: *Fairplay Flume*, Fairplay, Colorado, 1908-07-31.

## 1909: The Delaware Devil in Black

"Georgetown, Del. April 28. – More than seven feet in height and swathed in a long black cloak, closely wrapped around its face, a new mystery has been exciting some parts of Georgetown, where it has followed women and young girls and jumped out from behind trees at them. The 'Devil in Black,' as it is called, first appeared several nights ago, when a dozen or so persons saw it during the course of the evening. From behind a tree it jumped at Mrs. William Curdy and sent her screaming with freight into a neighbor's house, while a daughter of Joseph Carnel also was chased by the mysterious stranger until she fell almost fainting into Fred Rust's grocery store. The men of the neighborhood, informed of the affair, led by William Curdy, ran across fields, jumped fences and through back yards, with the 'Devil' but a few yards ahead of them, but, while crossing the big ditch known as the Savannah, the figure completely disappeared and, despite search, could not be found. Again it was seen by several young girls and last night it made its appearance and was seen closely by Mrs. Carn Josephs, who heard a noise as she passed her woodshed. She turned to look and distinctly saw the 'Devil' walk out of the shed and after her. Almost fainting with fear she ran screaming into the house, while her husband ran into the yard with his gun and fired at the tall figure, which was plainly distinguished at the woodshed. In a second it was gone with no trace of injury from the gun. Many superstitious declare that bullets cannot hit it, but some of the more determined men declare it is the work of a practical joker and expect to put a load of shot into it at their first opportunity."

Source: "Town Is Terrorized By A 'Devil In Black.' Mysterious Giant

Figure Keeps Georgetown, Del., Guessing – Appears at Night Before Women and Children. Superstitious Say It Can't Be Harmed by Bullets," *Washington Times*, Washington D.C., 1909-04-28.

## 1913: The Jesup, Spring Creek Valley invulnerable ghost

"The chain of mystery surrounding the purported appearance of a ghost at the home of William Kreuger, a farmer, residing near Jesup, has never been unravelled and bids fair to remain one of Spring Creek valley's unsolved problems. It will be recalled that the reported appearance of the ghost at the Kreuger home early in February had the entire western section of Buchanan county in a state of excitement. Mr. Kreuger while husking corn from the fodder one evening shortly after dark was confronted by a phantom-like figure that stood motionless and stolid. It was white as unsuned snow and immediately struck terror to his heart, so he says. When a reporter for the Courier called at the Kreuger home yesterday and inquired as to the present whereabouts of the 'ghost,' the Jesup farmer in a tremulous tone of voice declared that it had been almost two months since the strange phantom made its eighth appearance and that it has gone as mysteriously as it came. 'I feel certain it wasn't a spook,' declared Mr. Kreuger, 'for I never believed in spooks.' The strangest thing about its appearance was the fact that neither bullets nor buckshot could make any impression on it.... 'When I levelled the barrel of the gun and fired, the demon, ghost or whatever you want to call it was standing still and stolid. Crack went my rifle and I rushed up to claim my prey. Lo! It had suddenly disappeared. The next time "ghosty" came I used my shotgun with like results...'"

Sources: "Headless Ghost Defies Daylight, Powder and Lead," *Waterloo Evening Courier*, Waterloo, Iowa, 1913-02-14. "Never Feased By Rifle Shot. Ghost Seen By Farmer Was Bullet Proof. Neighborhood Near Jesup Startled By Mysterious Phantom," *Waterloo Evening Courier*, Waterloo, Iowa, 1913-03-24.

## 1916: The Goldfield, Nevada jumping ghost

"A galloping, jumping ghost, clad in skirts, appeared on the streets of Goldfield this week and Fred Moore, employed in the engineering department of the Consolidated Mines company, chased the apparition for several blocks, when it disappeared. Moore says he thinks the wearer of the ghostly attire was a man dressed in woman's clothes."

Source: *Nevada State Journal*, Reno, Nevada, 1916-07-15.

**1927: The Oakland black robed entity from the murder house**
"The people of Oakland are pretty well convinced that a house where a murder was committed last week is haunted. The experience of a certain electrician as recounted by the worthy A.P. was terrifying enough: John Smith, electrician, said he passed the murder house recently and a tall, heavy set man, garbed in a gown like a black kimono and wearing a 'strange looking thing on his head,' walked out and started after him. Smith said he ran as fast as he could."

Comment: It needs to be explained here that the house was the crime scene of the gruesome murder of the 15-year-old schoolgirl Mabel Mayer, a murder that got nationwide coverage and remains unsolved to this very day.

Sources: "The Horrible Experience Of Mr. John Smith," *Modesto News-Herald*, Modesto, California, 1927-07-06. The same item was also published a day later in the same newspaper. A reference to Smith's unsettling encounter is also found in "Oakland Girl Murdered By Maniac, Say Authorities. Slayer Believed Man of Perverted Mind; Run Down Clues." *Modesto News-Herald*, Modesto, California, 1927-07-06. "Suspect In jail For Questioning On Mabel Mayer. Charles Schlenker Arrested When He Appears At Hospital With Wounds. Oakland Police Find Rendezvous In Shed. Residence Where Girl Was Killed Now Branded As 'Spook House.'" *The Fresno Bee*, Fresno, California, 1927-07-06.


**THEO PAIJMANS** is a Dutch fortean researcher and the author of two books, one of which, *Free Energy Pioneer: John Worrell Keely*, has been published in English and Japanese. His articles have appeared in *Fortean Times, Gazette Forteenne, Bres, All Hallows,* and on any number of blogs. His email address is th.paijmans@wxs.nl.

# BETWEEN WORLDS:
## THE THREE NEPHITES
### By Loren Coleman

During the 2008 presidential campaign season there was much talk of Mormonism and The Church of Jesus Christ of Latter-Day Saints because of the candidacy of Mitt Romney, the former governor of Massachusetts. But few of those interested in his candidacy realized that one tenet of the Mormon faith includes the belief in a race of beings who live in a world between the known and unknown. The Church of Jesus Christ of Latter-Day Saints accept as true that the Nephites – initially righteous people, who eventually fell into wickedness – once existed and may still walk among us, saving lives and doing good deeds, and looking for redemption.

The Foundation for Ancient Research and Mormon Studies, part of Brigham Young University, performs extensive archeological research in search of evidence of the Nephites. Nevertheless, non-Mormon archaeologists have accepted no archaeological finding as evidence that Nephites existed or have any historical connection to Native Americans. Mormon researchers state that the lack of archaeological evidence to support the historicity of the Nephites (specifically, the lack of evidence for their cities and culture) is, in part, due to the current incomplete nature of archaeological studies of Meso-America in general, but they maintain that as further evidence is gathered, this situation may change.

It is with such a foundation that an unfolding of the deep history of the Nephites must be investigated in 2007-2008 America.

The back-story begins in the summer of 1494, on the occasion of Christopher Columbus' second voyage to the Americas. One day, while exploring the West Indies, Columbus anchored his ships off the coast of Cuba near a beautiful palm grove and sent a landing party to shore to get a fresh supply of wood and water. As others in the group cut wood and filled their water casks, an archer strayed into the forest with his crossbow in search of game, only to return a few minutes later to relate a baffling and frightening experience. The man, clearly shaken, reported that just a few moments before he had suddenly come upon a band of about thirty well-armed Indians, which was unsettling enough, but nothing compared to *the sight of three white men* who were in the company of the natives.

The white men, who wore white tunics that reached to their knees, immediately spotted the intruder, and as the Indians watched impassively, one of the three stepped toward the hunter and started to speak, when the hunter, giving vent to an understandable impulse, took to his heels and ran.

Upon hearing the story, Columbus' men – like their informant more frightened of the Indians than curious about the enigmatic white men – got on their boat and made with all haste back to the fleet. The next day Columbus dispatched another party to search for the strangers and the following day still another, but no trace of them was ever found, much to the admiral's frustration. Columbus was still laboring under the delusion that he was cruising the shoreline of Asia and believed that the three men might be inhabitants of the province Mangon.

Washington Irving, who recorded this peculiar incident in his *Life and Voyages of Christopher Columbus,* felt compelled to apologize for including it in his book and then, perhaps by way of penance, went on to offer his own imaginative explanation. "As no tribe of Indians was ever discovered in Cuba wearing clothing," he wrote, "it is possible that the story of the men in white originated in some error of the archer, who, full of the ideas of the mysterious inhabitants of Mangon, may have been startled in the course of his lonely wandering in the forest by one of those flocks of cranes which it seems abounded in the neighborhood."

Well, one can hardly blame Irving for trying, since there is no room in our conventional understanding of history for Caucasians co-existing with American Indians before Columbus' arrival. It is easier to believe in cranes that look like men than it is to deal with disquieting notions suggested by a number of unacceptable yet oddly consistent yarns, claims and folk tales about a trio of decidedly unusual gentlemen usually called the Three Nephites.

Let us skip over three centuries and move from Christopher Columbus in Cuba to one Joseph Smith of Palmyra, New York. Smith, born in 1805, died young (he and his brother Hyrum were done in by a lynch mob in Carthage, Illinois on June 27, 1844) but distinguished himself, and also brought on his murder, by founding the Church of the Latter-Day Saints, better known as the Mormon Church, under the alleged direction of angelic beings. The first supposed meeting with angels took place in 1820, when Smith was only 14. Several other visions occurred over the next few years, according to Smith, and led to his discovery on a hillside near Palmyra of gold plates, which detailed the alleged history of the former inhabitants of the North American continent. The plates disappeared after Smith "translated" them, but not before he had produced eleven witnesses to swear to their existence.

Whatever the truth about Smith's visions and the gold plates, there is no question that the resulting *Book of Mormon,* based on the prophet's translation, is a remarkable document probably quite beyond the inventive powers of the young man who was poorly educated and consequently not terribly literate. Attempts by skeptics since then to attribute the document to a reworking of an early 19th century romance by Solomon Spaulding have not been particularly successful. Moreover, Smith's sincerity is attested to by his refusal to recant his beliefs even in the face of the kind of savage persecution that finally ended in his death.

*The Book of Mormon* claims to be the record of the first inhabitants of the Western Hemisphere and covers a period from 600 B.C. to 400 A.D. It is made up of fourteen books and is more than five hundred pages long. The first two of these books, *I* and *II Nephi,* trace the flight of Lehi, a descendant of Joseph who was sold into Egypt by his brothers, and his family and followers from Jerusalem to a land of promise across the sea. Once there, two of the sons, Laman and Lemuel, led a rebellion against their father and were punished by being cursed with dark skin. From these Lamanites, says Mormon doctrine, the American Indians descended.

Another son, Nephi, remained faithful, however, and the major books of the *Book* follow the fortunes of the Nephites up to and beyond the coming of Christ to the continent after the Resurrection.

The chronicle concludes with the final battle between the Nephites and the Lamanites, which resulted in the decimation of the Nephites and in the prophet Moroni, Mormon's son, placing the gold plates at the site of the struggle, from there to be recovered centuries later by Joseph Smith.

Just how one chooses to take these revelations depends on how seriously one takes the doctrine of Mormonism. I am not Mormon, and I have my reservations. On the other hand, for reasons I am about to explain, I believe the answers – whatever and wherever they may be – are not likely to be simple; in fact, they may even be downright hair-raising. For Mormonism has given rise to one of the weirdest mysteries of American folklore.

In the book of *III Nephi* we are told the story of Christ's ministry in the New World, which in at least one important detail parallels the *New Testament's* account; namely, in Jesus' gathering about him twelve apostles. In the Book, however, three of these Nephite disciples ask that they be allowed to remain on Earth to continue their ministry until his return. Mormon makes reference to having seen these three (325 A.D.) and in the final part of the work, Moroni says that he too had dealings with them before the Lord withdrew them from the company of the later Nephites, who had degenerated into sinful unbelievers. "Whether they be upon the face of the land no man knoweth," Moroni wrote (Mormon 8: 11).

In the famous Christian legend of the Wandering Jew we also encounter the motif of the man who has traveled the world over preaching the gospel and whose labors will cease only at the Second Coming. Only in this case, the traveler has not made the choice; it has been forced on him by way of punishment because he scorned Jesus as he carried the cross to Cavalry.

A related legend, this one concerning St. John the Beloved, is apparently based on Christ's remark in Matthew 16:28: "Verily I say unto *you,* There be some standing here, which shall not taste of death, till they see the Son of man coming in his kingdom." As George K. Anderson observes in his definitive *The Legend of the Wandering Jew,* "Christ's statement seems to indicate his belief that the kingdom of God is to come within the lifetime of many in Christ's audience; it is not to be some divine, far-off event, but something to take place in the not distant future. If we leave aside this theological point, however, the actual interpretation of this remark by certain followers of Christ made it possible to read into the verse a promise of immortality, although this immortality might mean only a continuance on earth until such time as Christ returned with God's kingdom."

Out of these two traditions grew a large body of myth, lore, and literature that has fascinated students of human belief for centuries. In its usual form, tales of St. John and the Wandering Jew recount the appearance of a venerable old man with a long beard, a staff, and tattered clothes who preaches the word of God, effects miraculous cures, and rescues people in time of danger. These stories are incredibly widespread, or rather were, since they seem no longer to exist in folk tradition (the last recorded tale goes back to Utah of 1900). But in their time they ranged from Asia Minor to the New World.

An Indian legend from upstate New York serves as a bridge between the older myth and the relatively more recent Three Nephites tradition we are about to explore. The incident in question is supposed to have occurred in the late 18th or early 19th century at Hector Falls, near the town of Watkins. For some time the Indians had noted the presence of a mysterious figure, a white man, who was often seen traveling alone among the ravines and woodlands of the lake country. The Indians stayed out of his way, suspecting that he might be some kind of supernatural being who, if disturbed, could bring harm to the tribe. Finally one of them discovered that the man was a Jew. Not long afterwards the chiefs called a tribal council to discuss what they might do about the unwanted visitor.

By now their uneasiness about his presence had led to paranoid fears that he might be plotting to assassinate their queen, the semi-legendary Katharene, so they agreed to drive him out of the neighborhood. The next time they saw him; a group of warriors set off in hot pursuit and chased him until they had him cornered. Or so they thought. The stranger suddenly darted off in the direction of Hector Falls, but caught between the darkness and his own panic, he fell off a precipice, grasping at the last moment at the branches of a small tree to prevent him from plunging into the waters below. Unfortunately for him, the tree could not sustain his weight; it and he went down.

Though they searched for years, the Indians never found his body. To commemorate the event they marked the site of his fall with a white spot, known to this day as the "Painted Rock."

A legend, of course, and perhaps nothing more, but an interesting one in view of the fact that Mormonism in later years would take root in upstate New York, in the same area where, according to *The Book of Mormon,* the last battle between the Nephites and the Lamanites had taken place. The tale is all the more fascinating because, like the Cuban encounter discussed earlier, it predates Mormonism.

But if the story is only legend, the peculiar affair of Robert Edge is something more than that. That someone who called himself Edge actually existed is hardly open to doubt, since many people saw him and his activities were reported in local newspapers. But the implications may be a bit more than a 21st-century skeptic might feel comfortable having to contemplate.

On a calm, sunny day in May 1878, a clap of thunder resounded over a thirty-five-mile area encompassing Lexington, Tennessee, and the surrounding countryside. There was not a cloud in the sky and when no storm followed the thunder, residents of Henderson County were nonplussed. That afternoon, a stranger, described as about thirty years old, slender, of medium height, with fair skin, dark-brown curly hair, and a light reddish beard wandered into town and announced he would hold a religious service that night.

By evening the visitor had excited considerable controversy because even though no one had ever seen him before he seemed to know the area intimately. Rumors circulated that this man, who gave his name as Robert Edge, was someone special and so when the time came Lexington residents flocked to the meeting, hardly knowing what to expect.

What they got from Edge was a sermon unlike any they had heard before. Attacking the organized Christian churches as the "mother of harlots" (Smith's angelic informants called other churches "an abomination in his sight"), he called for a return to the principles of the primitive church, condemned secret societies, explained Biblical prophecies, and called on his listeners to prepare for the imminent Second Coming by abandoning all earthly concerns and giving themselves to Christ.

Many in the audience were deeply moved and before long Edge had gathered around him a respectable following. He roamed the country going to homes, farms and towns without ever having to ask for directions, a talent which contributed considerably to the aura of mystery around him. Individuals assigned to watch him complained that they could not keep track of him. Further, according to one account, "It was discovered that no one had ever seen him at any distance from a place of worship, and he was never seen until he arrived in the crowd or assumed his place in the pulpit." One rumor, which Edge would neither confirm nor deny, alleged that the enigmatic evangelist was a Mormon.

Determined to uncover the truth, a local Baptist deacon, named Jones, went to a house where Edge was eating and confronted him.

"My friend," Jones asked, "where are *you* from?"

"From about six miles," Edge answered evasively. He was referring to the town where he had been earlier in the day.

"What church do *you* belong to?"

"The church of God, sir."

"Where is it?"

"In the United States." (Mormons believe that America is the chosen land of God.)

"You have been speaking about one being ordained before he had the right to preach. By whom were *you* ordained?"

"By Jesus Christ, Sir."

"Where?"

"In Eternity."

"How long have *you* been preaching?"

"About 1,800 years."

At this point Jones left in disgust.

Edge is said to have had advance knowledge of dangers about to befall him and he managed to disappear somehow before an angry mob could locate him. He was never seen or heard from again. Later his followers joined the Mormon Church and, heeding Edge's advice to move West if they were subjected to persecution, escaped Henderson County and settled in Colorado.

Another mysterious stranger figures in an Augusta, Georgia

legend. Around 1890, Augusta citizens discovered a remarkable evangelist in their midst, an elderly man with neatly-trimmed white hair and of stately appearance, with a clear, pleasant voice that was "yet incisive even to the piercing of the human heart." Like Edge he revealed little if anything about himself and preached like the prophets of old, doing most of his speaking in the Market Place, a construction composed of two large sheds that extended about a hundred feet across the street and about two hundred feet in length. Pillars supported the sheds, known as the Upper and Lower Markets. Here farmers brought in food from their fields, and townspeople came to purchase their daily groceries.

One day the old man announced that a storm would destroy the Lower Market and leave only the southwest pillar standing to prove that he was a prophet of God. Anyone who tried to move the pillar would die, he said. Not long afterward, an electrical storm erupted; the Lower Market burned to the ground and only the southwest pillar remained. Later the evangelist visited at the home of Mr. and Mrs. Mack Little of Groveland, Georgia, fifteen miles west of Augusta. He repeated the prophecy once more before he left. Descendants of the Little family swore to the truth of the story many years later. The "Pillar of Prophecy" survived the great Augusta fire of 1916 and was still there as late as 1920.

Mormon patriarch David F. Fawns of Canada supplied his own footnote to the legend by claiming that on two occasions in 1900, as he stood by the pillar, the mysterious old man appeared to him. Fawns thought he might be one of the Three Nephites.

Now let us turn our attention to Utah, where in 1847 the Mormons established themselves after being driven out of the more settled regions of the country, and consider briefly what the participants took to be a miraculous visitation by a Nephite. The incident supposedly occurred in April 1852, in Salt Lake City.

One day during a long period of particular hardship for the newly arrived Mormons, an aged man knocked at the door of a local family and asked if he could eat with them. Food was scarce, but the wife gave him what she had, namely water, bread, and onions, which the stranger consumed quickly. When he had finished, he asked how much he owed her, jingling coins in his pocket to prove he could pay well. She refused the offer, at which point the stranger took two or three measured steps toward her and spoke in a voice so powerful that she almost fainted and had to sit down when she heard it.

"Well" he said, "if *you* charge me nothing for my dinner, may God bless *you* and peace be with *you.*"

The stranger turned and walked out. The wife asked a Mrs. Dunsdon, a neighbor who was there visiting at the time, to look out and see where the man was going. However, he had already disappeared and could not be found, even though in those early days there were no houses around, "not even an outhouse," the woman later wrote, "nor fence of any kind to intercept the *eye.*" Still more oddly, when she returned to clear the table, the food was still there as if it had not been touched at all!

She subsequently recalled how her family had survived the famine even when her neighbors were starving. She said they had even had enough food left over to feed others who were less fortunate. "I gave in the day of my poverty, of the scanty store I had to the man of God," she remarked, "and it seems that ever after, my meal sack was never empty."

During the summer of 1874, Mrs. Edwin Squires of Wa Wa Springs, Utah, played host to a mysterious visitor who appeared

Credit: Beth Fideler, Philip Hemstreet, and Loren Coleman

out of nowhere to ask for a meal. Before his arrival she had gone to the spring for water and studied the desolate area for signs of her husband, who was due at any moment. She saw no one coming, so she went inside, put the water down, turned around and was stunned to see a man with gray hair and a long white beard standing there. When he requested something to eat, she uneasily prepared him a meal, which he ate as though very hungry.

In the course of the meal he commented that she was not well.

"That's true," she said. "I have had a pain under my shoulder that has bothered me a great deal."

To which the old man replied, "Your liver is responsible for that, but it won't be bothering you any longer." Then he rose, thanked her and said, "God bless you, sister. You will never want for anything again. You will always be blessed with plenty."

Moments after he had walked out the door, Mrs. Squires stepped outside to see in which direction he had gone-only to discover that he had disappeared as suddenly as he had appeared.

Mrs. Squires came to believe her visitor was one of the Three Nephites. Her health problems ceased soon after her experience, as did the family's financial difficulties. When she died at the age of 89, her wealth was able to set all her children up in business.

So far, not one of our supposed Nephites has identified himself as such, unless one counts Edge's claim to having been around for 1,800 years as something as good as an admission. But in the summer of 1876 a peculiar white man named Nephi ministered to the Indians at Duck Creek, west of St. George, Utah. Nephi, who sported a long white beard and dressed himself entirely in white, told the Indians that the Mormons were their friends and would show them a better life. He also maintained that he was one of their forefathers and had been on earth for hundreds and hundreds of years. During the whole of his stay not a single Indian was seen along the nearby Virgin River or any of its tributaries.

Two women, one a Mormon, the other an atheist, who joined the Latter-Day Saints after the experience, credited one of the Three Nephites with saving their lives. One evening in the summer of 1900 they became trapped on a mountainside when their horses refused to cross a crevice filled with shale. The animals had panicked when the shale began to slide and would move neither backward nor forward. Maud May Babcock, the Mormon lady, dismounted and crawled over the mountaintop in hopes of running into a wandering prospector. When that did not happen, she made her way back with a small willow and tried to drive the horse with it, but he still would not move. Finally, every other option exhausted, she prayed.

Suddenly a voice from above her asked, "How did you come here, my daughter?"

As Miss Babcock was to write, "I jabbered in my relief and excitement, trying to explain our predicament, and before my explanation was finished I was standing on the top with Miss Carrie Helen Lamson and both our horses in a circle facing the stranger." She had no idea how they had gotten there.

Their mysterious helper had a gray Vandyke beard, wore a cap on his head and was dressed in blue overalls. He looked well scrubbed and his soft white hands appeared unused to hard manual labor. When he spoke he addressed Miss Babcock as "my daughter," when Miss Lamson, the non-Mormon, would ask him a question, he would direct his answer to her companion.

As they talked with him, the two women mounted their horses and prepared to resume their journey. They set off and had not gone more than twenty feet when Miss Babcock realized she had not thanked him for his help. She turned around and discovered, much to her astonishment, that he was gone. Since they had clear vision for at least a mile in every direction she could only conclude that he had vanished.

"He was one of the Three Nephites," she exclaimed suddenly.

Another, more circumstantial tale was told by John Alfred of Salt Lake City, who recounted an alleged experience that took place as he lay under an elm tree waiting for services to begin at the Mormon Temple. I mention it not because it is documented (it isn't), but because it has a Nephite identifying himself as such and also because it connects the Nephite tradition with a legend discussed earlier.

"A man came walking up-a long, white-bearded man," Alfred said. "He walked up to me and shook hands with me. He said, 'I want you to know you have met and shaken hands with one of the "Apostles of Jesus Christ, ordained by the hand of Jesus Christ himself more than 2,000 years ago.' He told me the various things he had seen, the places he had been, things that had transpired over a period of 2,000 years. He had thrilled as he saw the church grow, and told me what it had meant to him personally because of the many defenses that had been given. He mentioned a pillar in Augusta, Georgia."

These incidents, or alleged incidents, are fairly typical of the hundreds told in past years about the Nephites. As a general rule, the three were not seen together, did not identify themselves directly (although in rare instances one would say, "I am one of the Three"), appeared and disappeared miraculously, made prophecies and seemed to know all things.

Usually it was Mormons who encountered them, though that was not invariably the case. In some few instances only certain persons saw them. They appeared to all kinds of people, not just the gullible and superstitious. A. E. Fife, who collected a large variety of Nephite stories for a study of the subject in *The Journal of American Folk-Lore,* noted that a number of those he interviewed "were trained college people, among whom were medical men, college professors, and other professional people."

The problem folklorists have encountered in attempting to explain the persistent Nephite legends and reports is suggested by the conclusion Fife drew. "From the facts that we have gathered," he wrote, "it would seem that the Mormon converts who had certainly brought popular versions of the Wandering Jew legend to Utah with them, soon transformed them into Three Nephites legends once they had been exposed to the theology of Joseph Smith."

That would be true if the Three Nephites existed only as yams passed from person to person and from generation to generation. But, when one has to deal with personal experiences of others, then the question becomes infinitely more difficult. Fife does not dispute the sincerity of his informants, many of them devout Mormons, nor does he explain just how they managed to delude themselves into believing they had experienced something they hadn't. Hector Lee, another student of the legend, begs the question when he dismisses first-hand testimony as, although not deliberately fabricated, "somehow psychic" – presumably meaning psychological.

Without committing myself to belief in 2,000-year old apostles (in which, lest readers mistake my meaning, I wish to emphasize I most decidedly do not believe), I think it is fairly obvious that folklorists simply do not care to confront the dazzling paranormal implications of the legend. The probably feel much the same way as the astronomer who a few years ago advanced a rather improbable "natural" explanation for a UFO sighting, remarking that while his theory might sound implausible it would have to do since flying saucers do not exist.

I would suggest a third alternative: namely, that Nephites as such do not exist, but that manifestations calling themselves or being taken for Nephites do. Thus, they join the ranks of supposed spirits of the dead, Venusians, visions of the Virgin Mary, which apparently exist but not as what they appear to be or say they are. What the purpose of this deception might be, I hesitate to speculate.

The Swedish mystic Emanuel Swedenborg, who recognized the illusory nature of these elemental forces in the 18th century, wrote the following from his own experience:

"When spirits begin to speak with a man, he must beware that he believe nothing that they say. For nearly everything they say is fabricated by them, and they lie: for if they are permitted to narrate anything, as what heaven is and how things in the heavens are to be understood, they would tell so many lies that a man would be astonished. This they would do with solemn affirmation. Wherefore men must beware, and not believe them. It is on this account that the state of speaking with spirits on this earth is most perilous."

Whatever the real story behind American manifestations of the Three Nephites, there can be no doubt that the many reports of these mysterious wanderers force us to have questions. For some in the American West today, as well, continued sightings of good Samaritans, who disappear after their good deeds, keep alive the Nephite tradition.

**LOREN COLEMAN** is a well-known cryptozoologist and fortean. He blogs regularly for *Cryptomundo*. He has also written many books, the latest of which is a reprint of his classic work, *Mysterious America*, published by Paraview Pocket Books in 2007. This article is an updated version of a chapter that appeared in the original edition of *Mysterious America,* but does not appear in the latest edition of the book.

# THE FLYING SAUCER THAT NEVER WAS
## BY NICK REDFERN

Born in Columbus, Ohio, on July 30, 1919, Mikel Conrad began to carve out a career for himself in Hollywood's movie world when he secured a small role in the 1947 production *Untamed Fury*, in which he played the memorably named Gator-Bait Blair. No less than twenty-three other movies followed, including 1948's *The Man from Colorado* that saw Conrad acting alongside leading actors of the day, William Holden and Glenn Ford. Twelve months later, Conrad made an on-screen appearance in *Abbott and Costello Meet the Killer: Boris Karloff*. He also starred with Tony Curtis in *Francis*, a 1950 comedy about a talking mule. But it was the sci-fi movie, *The Flying Saucer*, also released in 1950, that was Conrad's crowning glory, for the prime reason that it attracted the Top Secret attention of none other than the United States Air Force.

The storyline of *The Flying Saucer* that Conrad starred in, produced, directed, and co-wrote with Howard Irving Young, is an intriguing one: American secret agents discover that Russian spies have recently started to explore an otherwise unremarkable area of the Alaskan Territory. Their quarry: the mysterious flying saucers that had been invading the skies of our planet since 1947. The American agents manage to persuade a rich playboy named Mike Trent, portrayed by Conrad, to accompany a United States

Secret Service employee to the area in an effort to understand why the Soviets are so intensely interested in flying saucers.

To the surprise and delight of Trent, he finds that the Secret Service agent is a beautiful woman, Vee Langley, played by actress Pat Garrison. They quickly head off in hot pursuit of the truth, with Conrad's character pretending to be suffering from a nervous breakdown, while Langley assumes the role of his nurse. The two subsequently makes their way to Trent's cabin in the wilds of Alaska, where a caretaker named Hans, who has a distinctly foreign accent that sounds suspiciously Russian in nature, meets them.

Trent is certain that the whole UFO controversy is complete and utter nonsense – that is, until one soars across the skies near the cabin. The story then takes an intriguing turn when Hans's cover is blown and he is shown to be an undercover Soviet Intelligence agent. Meanwhile, the UFO is revealed to be not an alien spacecraft, but the product of a traitorous American scientist who has sold the secrets of his revolutionary aerial invention to the Kremlin.

Eventually, Trent and Langley capture the Red agents, locate the Soviets' secret flying saucer base, and finally watch the ship less-than-spectacularly explode in mid-air as a Russian spy vainly attempts to fly it to the Soviet Union.

It must be said that *The Flying Saucer* was hardly a classic, the special-effects leave a *lot* to be desired, and the movie vanished into obscurity shortly after its release, which surely begs the question: why would the United States' military take such an interest in Conrad's far from impressive foray into the world of sci-fi? The answer is quite simple: When *The Flying Saucer* was still in production, Conrad began spreading rumors in Hollywood, and with several media outlets in his home state of Ohio, to the effect that the movie would contain not special-effects footage of a UFO, but genuine, and highly spectacular, film of a *real* flying saucer in action.

At the time, the Air Force was deeply involved in trying to determine the truth that lay at the heart of the UFO mystery, and between 1948 (the year that saw the creation of the Air Force's first UFO program, *Project Sign* that was shortly afterwards replaced by *Project Grudge*) and 1969 (the year in which its final study, *Project Blue Book*, was closed down) the Air Force officially investigated 12,618 reported UFO sightings, of which 701 remained unexplained. And so, given that Conrad was making startling claims to the effect that he was in possession of stunning footage of genuine flying saucers, it is of little surprise that the Air Force secretly began looking into the man's activities and his claims.

The saga all began on September 14, 1949, when journalist Aline Mosby wrote an article titled "Film Actor Finds Flying Disc, But Press Agent Doubts Tale" that appeared in the Dayton, Ohio *Journal Herald* newspaper. Mosby's article told a story that, if true, was startling, to say the very least.

The article began:

> Having taken care of rocket ships, atomic bombs and Superman, Hollywood now is starring a flying saucer in a movie. The Army's latest decision was there isn't any such thing, but this has not dampened the spirit of actor Mikel Conrad. He is acting in, producing, directing and writing *The Secret of the Flying Saucers*. The star, he insists, is a whirling disc, or reasonable facsimile thereof. The movie is a spy mystery which also features a blond heroine, a handsome hero and Russians as the villains.

Mosby then turned her attention to the most significant aspect of the story: the apparent acquisition by Conrad of real footage of flying saucers that he was supposedly going to reveal to the world in his sci-fi movie.

> The actor got this colossal idea, he says, while on location in Alaska last winter for a Universal-International movie, *Arctic Manhunt*. "I heard about flying saucers there so I went back last summer with a camera crew from Whitehorse (Canada) and two players, Pat Garrison and Hans von Teuffen," he says. "I found a saucer, I'm not telling how," a claim not believed even by one of his press agents.

The article further quoted Conrad as stating: "I have scenes of the saucer landing, taking off, flying and doing tricks. The saucer is not created in miniature or by trick photography. It is a mechanical, man-made object." Mosby then continued:

> Whether it is a dishpan sailing across the camera or some garage-made contraption, he won't say. Conrad and crew shot silent footage for three months. He'll begin shooting interior scenes and dubbing in sound Sept. 26, he says.

Notably, and somewhat tellingly, Mosby added: "His press agents have seen part of the film. They report it has some nice avalanches. They did not see any flying saucers."

According to Mosby's feature, Conrad had an answer for this latter point: "The saucer footage is locked in a bank vault. I'm not showing it to anyone yet."

There then followed a brief account of the movie's plot:

> The plot concerns a playboy, Michael Trent (Conrad), who steels his weak chin and goes saucer-hunting in Alaska for the government. To throw Russian spies off his track, he cleverly disguises himself as a drunkard seeking the cure. Trent is accompanied by an FBI agent, who turns out to be a beautiful blond (Miss Garrison), cleverly disguised as his nurse.

Conrad told Mosby: "We get snowbound in a remote cabin and romance finds a way."

Mosby seemed less than impressed by Conrad, his sensational claims, and his then-forthcoming movie, as her closing words noted: "Will Michael and Violet get out of the cabin before they're trapped by snow? Or the Russians? Or the Saucers? Will they capture the saucer? Will they drop dead before the end of the movie? Will you?"

Two days later, staff at the Air Technical Intelligence Center (ATIC) at Wright-Patterson Air Force Base, which was deeply involved in the investigation of UFO sightings at the time, recorded in an internal memo that details of Aline Mosby's article had been brought to their attention. Interestingly, however, ATIC officials noted that Conrad was claiming his forthcoming movie was being made "with the permission of authorities." Indeed, this specific statement related to the fact that Conrad had the audacity to hire an actor friend to pose as an official of the FBI, thus creating the impression that J. Edgar Hoover's finest had somehow assisted in – or contributed to –the making of *The Flying Saucer*. At the time, however, the Air Force did not know this was nothing more than one of Conrad's cunning, and completely bogus, publicity schemes.

Copy

5D-OSI/JCS/smb

5D-24-21DD                                          27 September 1949

SUBJECT: FLYING DISCS - Alleged observation
          of flying discs by MIKEL CONRAD
          during winter of 1948/49 in
          Territory of Alaska.

TO:      Acting District Commander
          13th OSI District (IO)
          822nd USAF Specialized Depot
          P. O. Box 215
          Maywood, California

   1. Transmitted herewith for your information, facsimile of newspaper clipping extracted from 14 September 1949 issue of the "Journal-
Herald", published in Dayton, Ohio, wherein, under by-line of ALINE
MOSBY, Hollywood, dated 13 September 1949, it is alleged that one,
        , did, during the winter of 1948/49 in Alaska, observe so-
called "flying saucers", located one of same and took motion pictures
of cited saucers in various flight stages and manoeuvers.

   2. Request appropriate investigation be conducted by your district
in accordance with provisions of AFOSI Letter No. 85, dated 12 August
1949.

   3. For the purpose of this investigation, it is requested that the
title to be used in the preparation of Report of Investigation be as
indicated above.

   4. Request Report of Investigation be submitted this office,
in six copies, so that this office may comply with Paragraph 3e(1),(2),
(4), of cited AFOSI Letter.

   5. In the event investigation has already been initiated, by your
office, covering incident referred to in title; it is requested instructions
contained in above paragraphs be ignored and six copies of investigation
furnished this district.

Incl:                            JAMES F. X. O'CONNELL
 Facsimile of newspaper          Lt Colonel, USAF
 clipping extracted from         District Commander
 14 Sep 49 issue of
 "Journal-Herald" (in trip)

Copy

As a result of the growing interest in Conrad's movie, in September 1949, Lt. Colonel James F. X. O'Connell, District Commander with the Air Force Office of Special Investigations prepared a confidential memorandum for the attention of the Acting District Commander of the 18th OSI District, 822nd USAF Specialized Dept, at Maywood, California. Titled "FLYING DISCS – Alleged observation of flying discs by MIKEL CONRAD during winter if 1948/49 in Territory of Alaska," it reads thus:

> 1. Transmitted herewith for your information, facsimile of newspaper clipping extracted from 14 September 1949 issue of the "Journal-Herald" published in Dayton, Ohio, wherein, under by-line of ALINE MOSBY, Hollywood, dated 13 September 1949, it is alleged that one, Mikel Conrad did, during the winter of 1948.49 in Alaska, observe so-called "flying saucers", located one of same and took motion pictures of cited saucers in various flight stages and maneuvers.
>
> 2. Request appropriate investigation be conducted by your district.
>
> 3. For the purpose of this investigation, it is requested that the title to be used in the preparation of Report of Investigation be as indicated above.
>
> 4. Request Report of Investigation be submitted to this office, in six copies.
>
> 5. In the event investigation has already been initiated, by your office, covering incident referred to in title; it is requested instructions contained in above paragraphs be ignored and six copies of investigation furnished this district.

Evidently, the matter was taken seriously at an official level, as various elements of the Air Force were implicated in the investigation of Conrad's controversial claims and *The Flying Saucer* for the next two months. A November 12, 1949, confidential Air Force report summarizes the "facts" pertaining to this strange affair. The first paragraph of the document reveals that the Air Force had heard additional rumors to the effect that not only was Conrad in possession of film footage of UFOs, but that he had nothing less than an actual flying saucer "in his possession."

> On 20 September 1949, the 5th OSI District Office, Wright-Patterson AFB, was requested by Lt. Col. A.J. HEMSTREET, JR., Acting Chief, Analysis Division, Intelligence Department, Hq., AMC [Air Materiel Command], to initiate an investigation for the purpose of confirming or denying the allegations made by one MIKEL CONRAD, wherein he claimed to have in his possession a "flying saucer," as well as various scenes showing the alleged saucers landing and taking off. As a result of this request the 5th OSI District Office prepared a letter to the 18th OSI District Office, Maywood, California, requesting that appropriate investigation of this matter be conducted in the Hollywood area.
>
> On 17 October 1949, 5th District was informed by Lt Col H.W. POTE, Deputy Chief, Public Information Office, Hq. AMC, Wright-Patterson AFB, that he had received a telephone call from Lt J.G. MORRIS, Public Relations Office, Hq. USAF, Washington, D.C., advising that his (MORRIS) office was in receipt of a telephone call from [Deleted] the Editor of "Film Daily" and that he had received a press release from one MIKEL CONRAD to the effect that he CONRAD had in his possession 900 feet of film about "flying saucers" in Alaska; that [Deleted] requested any information available as to the authenticity of CONRAD'S material and whether an investigation had been conducted of subject

matter. Lt MORRIS asked Colonel POTE whether Wright Field investigated the subject matter and for any information available concerning CONRAD.

Air Force documentation shows that Pote then contacted Lt. H.W. Smith, the project officer with Project Grudge at the Air Technical Intelligence Center at Wright-Patterson Air Force Base, who advised Pote that he was personally unaware of such an investigation. Smith was careful to add, however, that if Wright-Patterson *was* involved, then it was likely that its Office of Special Investigations (OSI) would have been the specific office implicated, and that he, Smith, would have been kept out of the loop with respect to any such secret inquiries.

INTERMEDIATE STATES

A Freedom of Information Act Request has shown that an extensive investigation of Mikel Conrad and his fantastic claims *did* proceed, and that it was specifically conducted by elements of the 18ᵗʰ OSI District. Evidence of this can be found in the following report of November 22, 1949:

> A report subsequently submitted by the 18ᵗʰ OSI DO [District Office] dated 3 November 1949 stated that after some investigation in an effort to locate MIKEL CONRAD, it was determined that he was presently an actor-producer-writer in Los Angeles, California. When contacted CONRAD informed OSI Agent SHILEY that his picture "The Flying Saucer" was to be previewed by the censors of the [Deleted] office in Hollywood, and invited Agent SHILEY to attend the showing after which, he suggested, the Agent could question him concerning the "saucer."

As the following, final extract from the document indicates, Conrad decided to come clean to Agent Shiley, and he admitted that his story about having filmed real flying saucers was nothing more than a fabrication designed to generate publicity for his movie. Possibly, with the Air Force now asking questions, Conrad was concerned that legal action might follow, and this was an attempt on his part to appease the military and prevent matters from escalating to a more serious level. And the fact that Conrad had even enlisted a friend to pose as a special agent of the FBI makes his confession even more understandable. The report states:

> Agent SHILEY attended the preview of CONRAD'S movie on 26 October 1949, and after the showing CONRAD indicated that the "flying saucer was a figment of his imagination," and stated that he had released the story in order to advertise his picture. He admitted that the alleged observation, location, and the motion picture of the "flying

saucer" in various flight stages and maneuvers was not a reality.

CONRAD apologized to Agent SHILEY for the story which appeared in the press and said he was sorry that he had misled the USAF, and admitted that the article was purely for enhancing interest in his coming picture. He requested that the USAF not furnish any newspaper correspondent or other persons making inquiries with the fact that the "saucer is a hoax." CONRAD was advised that OSI would not because OSI had no interest in his picture, since he had not actually sighted any unconventional object in the sky.

And, thus, one of the stranger – and certainly surreal – episodes in the early years of the Air Force's UFO investigations was brought to a close. But an intriguing question remains: Why was the Air Force so keen to determine the truth behind Conrad's claims that he had genuine footage of UFOs in flight in his possession? If the Air Force thought UFOs were not worthy of investigation, it would surely have avoided expending both valuable manpower and money on investigating Conrad's story. Yet investigate it, the Air Force did, even to the extent of ensuring that an agent of the OSI was firmly in place at the first, private viewing of *The Flying Saucer*.

Perhaps we should consider the possibility that the seriousness and diligence shown by the Air Force in investigating Conrad and his sci-fi movie stemmed from the fact that the military, itself, knew that UFOs existed because the military was already in possession of top secret films like those Conrad asserted he possessed. It would be truly ironic if Conrad's lies and distortions had actually touched upon a very *real*, and highly classified, official story concerning genuine secrets of flying saucers in Alaska. And, incredibly, that may have been precisely what happened.

Formerly classified FBI files tell of startling UFO encounters in Alaska in the period 1947-1950 – and it is not at all out of the question that at least some of the 1947 cases, in particular, may have been the ones that Conrad claimed knowledge of to journalist

Aline Mosby in 1949. More interesting is the fact that another flurry of UFO activity kicked off in Alaska in January 1950 – just three months after AFOSI agent Shiley got to see an advance-screening of *The Flying Saucer*, and just before the movie hit the big-screen.

In August of 1947 the FBI in Anchorage received a highly impressive account of a UFO incident involving two serving members of the military. The report read: "This is to advise that two army officers reported to the Office of the Director of Intelligence Headquarters Alaskan Department, at Fort Richardson, Alaska, that they had witnessed an object passing through the air at a tremendous rate of speed which could not be judged as to miles per hour."

According to the official report, the UFO was initially sighted by only one of the two officers, but he soon alerted his colleague to the strange sight.

> The object appeared to be shaped like a sphere and did not give the impression of being saucer-like or comparable to a disk. The first officer stated that it would be impossible to give minute details concerning the object, but that it appeared to be approximately two or three feet in diameter and did not leave any vapor trail in the sky.

Experienced officer that he was, he first attempted to gauge the altitude of the object, and, from a comparison with cloud formations in the area, he determined that whatever the nature of the mystery sphere, it was cruising at a height of more than ten thousand feet. And it should be noted that to be at such a height and still be visible, in all probability the UFO must have exceeded the initial size estimation of "two or three feet" by a considerable degree.

When questioned, the second officer gave a substantially similar account, the only marked difference being that, in his opinion, he considered the object to have been approximately ten feet in diameter, and compared it to "half the size of a full moon on an ordinary night." This discrepancy in size was apparently due to the fact that the second officer believed the UFO was more likely to have been at a height of three-to-four thousand feet, rather than at an altitude of ten thousand feet as had been suggested by his colleague.

The difference of opinion over the altitude and size of the object may or may not have been significant; the important factor, however, was that both officers agreed that they had most definitely seen some type of anomalous object. And as the report concluded: "...the second officer pointed out that one of the remarkable features of this report was that it was definitely traveling against the wind."

Shortly afterwards, the FBI Office at Anchorage reported to Bureau Director J. Edgar Hoover that: "...we have been able to locate a flyer [who] observed some flying object near Bethel, Alaska in July 1947."

The report to Hoover continued:

> [The pilot] related that the occasion of seeing the flying object near Bethel was on a July day when the sky was completely clear of clouds, and it being during the early part, it is daylight the entire night. The time of his sighting this flying object was about 10 PM and the sun had just dropped beyond the horizon. Flying weather was extremely good and he was coming into the Bethel Airport with a DC-3.

On approaching the airport the pilot was amazed to see to his left an unidentified craft, "the size of a C-54 without any fuselage," which seemed to resemble a "flying wing." As a result of its unique shape, the pilot was initially unable to determine whether the object was heading towards his aircraft or away from it, and elected to make a forty-five-degree turn in an attempt to avoid any possiblity of collision. The FBI noted that the pilot was certain that the craft was free of any external power source, such as a propeller-driven engine, and exhibited no exhaust as it flew by. The document added:

> He called on his radio to the Civil Aeronautics Administration station at Bethel, asking what aircraft was in the vicinity and they had no reports of any aircraft. The object he sighted was some five or ten miles from the airport before his arrival and [he]

stated that the path did not go directly across the airport. He, of course, could not tell whether the object was making any noise and stated that it was flying at a thousand foot altitude and estimated travel at 300 miles per hour. It was traveling in the direction from Bethel to Nome, which is in a northwesterly direction. He noted no radio interference and is unable to describe the color other than it appeared dark but of definite shape and did not blend into the sky but had a definite, concise outline. [He] clearly observed the object at this time.

As the 1940s drew to a close and a new decade dawned, the FBI continued to receive and log high-quality UFO reports on a regular basis. Of those, one of the more credible sightings related to a noteworthy series of encounters that occurred in Alaskan airspace over the course of two days in early 1950.

Forwarded to the FBI by an official U.S. Navy source, the confidential three-page intelligence report paints a startling picture of multiple UFO encounters involving the military. Titled "Unidentified Phenomena in Vicinity of Kodiak, Alaska," it concerns "a report of sightings of unidentified airborne objects, by various naval personnel, on 22 and 23 January 1950."

> ...at 220240W January Lt. Smith, USN, patrol plane commander of P2V3 No. 4 of Patrol Squadron One reported an unidentified radar contact 20 miles north of the Naval Air Station, Kodiak, Alaska. When this contact was first made, Lt. Smith was flying the Kodiak Security Patrol. At 0243W, 8 minutes later a radar contact was made on an object 10 miles southeast of NAS Kodiak. Lt. Smith checked with the control tower to determine known traffic in the area, and was informed that there was none. During this period, the radar operator, Gaskey, ALC, USN, reported intermittent radar interference of a type never before experienced. Contact was lost at this

time, but intermittent interference continued.

Smith and Gaskey were not the only two to report that unidentified vehicles had intruded into Alaskan airspace. At the time of the their encounter, the *USS Tilbrook* was anchored in the vicinity of "buoy 19" in the nearby man ship channel. On board the *Tilbrook* was a seaman named Morgan (first name unknown) who was standing watch. At some point between 0200 and 0300 hours, Morgan reported that a "very fast moving red light, which appeared to be of exhaust nature seemed to come from the southeast, moved clockwise in a large circle in the direction of, and around Kodiak and returned out in a generally southeast direction."

Perhaps not quite believing what he was seeing, Morgan alerted one of his shipmates, Carver, to the strange spectacle, and both watched as the UFO made a "return flight." According to the testimony of Morgan and Carver: "The object was in sight for an estimated 30 seconds. No odor or sound was detected, and the object was described to have the appearance of a ball of fire about one foot in diameter."

A later portion of the report records yet another encounter with the mystery visitor: "At 220440W, conducting routine Kodiak security patrol, Lt. Smith reported a visual sighting of an unidentified airborne object at a range of 5 miles, on the starboard bow. This object showed indications of great speed on the radar scope. The trailing edge of the blip gave a tail like indication."

Lieutenant Smith quickly advised the rest of the crew of the PV23 No. 24 that the UFO was in sight, and all watched fascinated as the strange vehicle soared overhead at a speed estimated to have been around 1,800 mph. Smith climbed to intercept the UFO and vainly tried to circle it. Needless to say, its high speed and remarkable maneuverability ensured that Smith's actions resulted in complete failure. However, neither Lieutenant Smith nor his crew was quite prepared for what happened next: "Subsequently the object seemed to be opening the range," the official report reads, "and Smith attempted to close the range. The UFO was observed to open out somewhat, then to turn to the left and come up on Smith's quarter. Smith considered this to be a highly threatening gesture, and turned out all lights in the aircraft. Four minutes later the object disappeared from view in a southeasterly direction."

At 0435 hours on the following day, Lieutenants Barco and Causer of Patrol Squadron One were conducting the Kodiak Security Patrol when they, too, sighted an unidentified aerial vehicle. At the time of their encounter the aircraft in which the officers were flying was approximately 62 miles south of Kodiak. For ten minutes, Barco and Causer, along with the pilot, Captain Paulson, watched stunned as the mysterious object twisted and turned in the Alaskan sky. An assessment of these reports read thus:

> 1. To Lt. Smith and crew it appeared as two orange lights rotating about a common center, "like two jet aircraft making slow rolls in tight formation." It had a wide speed range.

> 2. To Morgan and Carver, it appeared as a reddish orange ball of fire about one foot in diameter, traveling at a high rate of speed.

> 3. To Causer, Barco and Paulson, it appeared to be a pulsating orange yellow projectile shaped flame, with regular periods of pulsation on 3 to 5 seconds. Later, as the object increased the range, the pulsations appeared to increase to on 7 or 8 seconds and off 7 to 8 seconds.

The final comment on the encounters reads: "In view of the fact that no weather balloons were known to have been released within a reasonable time before the sightings, it appears that the object or objects were not balloons. If not balloons the objects must be regarded as phenomena (possibly meteorites), the exact nature of which could not be determined by this office."

The "meteorite" theory for this series of encounters is particularly puzzling. It goes without saying that meteorites do not stay in sight for "an estimated 30 seconds;" meteorites do not close in on military aircraft in what is deemed to be a "highly threatening gesture;" and they do not appear as "two orange lights rotating about a common center." In other words, it seems safe to conclude that whatever it was, it was certainly not a meteorite.

And the story is still not quite over. In his 1997 book *Remote Viewing*, Jim Schnabel recounts the story of the U.S. Intelligence community's involvement in the controversial issue of psychic-spying that largely began in the early-to-mid 1970s. Commenting on the skills of a talented remote-viewer, Pat Price, Schnabel noted that Price said that "Alaska's Mount Hayes, the jewel of a glacial range northeast of Anchorage, housed one of the aliens' largest bases." According to Price, the aliens that lived deep inside Mount Hayes were very human-looking, with the only major differences being in their heart, lungs, blood and eyes. Ominously, he added that the aliens use "thought transfer for motor control of us."

"The site has also been responsible for strange activity and malfunction of U.S. and Soviet space objects," added Price.

We may never know for sure if it was these, and perhaps other, official UFO reports from Alaska that prompted the Air Force to take so much interest in the activities and spurious claims of Mikel Conrad. But of one thing we *can* be certain: The military's secret surveillance of Conrad, as he sought to bring *The Flying Saucer* to life, was certainly the highlight of his career. Several more movie roles followed, including a low-budget sci-fi picture from 1952 called *Untamed Women*, which (believe me) is far less exciting than its title suggests, and the 1956 production of *Godzilla, King of the Monsters*. After that, Conrad largely vanished into obscurity. Long forgotten, just like his masterpiece *The Flying Saucer*, Conrad died in poverty in Los Angeles on September 11, 1982.

**Sources**
*Remote Viewers*, Jim Schnabel, Bantam Doubleday Dell Publishing Group, 1997.
*The Flying Saucer*, <en.wikipedia.org/wiki/The_Flying_Saucer>.
*Film Actor Finds Flying Disc, But Press Agent Doubts Tale*, Dayton, Ohio *Journal Herald*, September 14, 1949.
*Remote Viewing Underground UFO Bases*, Cassandra 'Sandy' Frost, <www.rense.com>, November 28, 2005.

U.S. Air Force and FBI documentation (various, 1947-1950).


**NICK REDFERN** is the author of ten books on various aspects of Forteana, including *On the Trail of the Saucer Spies, Strange Secrets, Three Men Seeking Monsters*, and his latest title, *Memoirs of a Monster Hunter*. Nick writes regularly for *Fate, Fortean Times* and the British *Daily Express* newspaper. He can be contacted at his website: <www.nickredfern.com>.

# THEY DINE AMONG US
## By Cliff Willett

**Starters**

Our gods, it seems, have always been hungry gods, forever demanding their fair share of food, wine, and blood. The blood sacrifices of the Aztecs and the polite harvest festivals of rural England are merely variations of the same underlying ritual – that of expressing gratitude to the gods by gifting them a portion of the fruits of their fecundity.

Long into the modern Christian era, European country dwellers continued to offer food to the old deities in their diminished form as the good people, or fairy folk. "Food-sacrifice plays a very important role in the modern Fairy-Faith," wrote W. Evans Wentz in his classic 1911 study *The Fairy Faith in Celtic Countries*. "Without any doubt it is a survival from pagan times, when propitiatory offerings were regularly made to the Tuatha De Danann as gods of the earth, and, apparently, to other orders of spiritual beings."

Wentz went on to explain that the good people fed "not on the gross substance of food, but on its finer invisible essences." Three centuries earlier, clergyman Robert Kirk addressed the same topic in *The Secret Commonwealth*. Kirk believed that fairies were "of a middle nature betwixt man and Angel," with bodies "so pliable… that they can make them appear or disappear at pleasure." Some subsisted "by sucking into some fine spirituous essence that appears like pure air or oil." Others fed "upon the core substance of corn and liquor, or on corn itself that grows on the surface of the Earth; which these fairies do steal away as do crows and mice."

While fairies were quite capable of feeding themselves, they were nevertheless swift to punish mortals who failed to make symbolic offerings of food to them, however small. A farmer who failed to appease the gentry risked finding his crops blighted or his animals struck dead overnight. In more recent times, UFO activity has often been associated with both crop damage and cattle mutilations. Moreover, UFOs frequently leave patches of blighted earth behind them where, it is claimed, nothing will grow.

## Food of the Gods

A case in point is that of Maurice Masse, a French farmer who encountered a pair of otherworldly entities in his lavender fields one July morning in 1965. They arrived, appropriately enough, in an egg-shaped craft – the egg being universally recognized as a symbol of fertility. Equally appropriately, they were dressed in green. The four-foot-tall beings busied themselves picking lavender, or rather – to use the approved pseudoscientific terminology of UFOlogy – they busied themselves taking plant samples.

All might have gone well for Masse had he been content to let them let them take their share. Instead, he marched up to them intending to order them off his land. It was only when one of them spun around and paralyzed him with a tube-shaped device (the "fairy stroke" of old) that he fully realized the strangeness of the situation. He was unable to move for a quarter of an hour after the little humanoids had departed. The patch of ground where they had landed remained barren for a full decade after the visitation.

The trio of small fairy-like beings who visited housewife Jean Hingley early in January 1979 was granted a rather more cordial reception. They soared into her living room on butterfly-shaped wings and began shaking the Christmas tree while excitedly gabbling, "Nice? Nice?" Hingley, a devout Christian, wondered if they might be some peculiar breed of angel and asked if Jesus had sent them. "We know all about Jesus," they chorused in reply. "We came down here to talk to people, but they don't seem to be interested!"

In the spirit of the season, Hingley offered each of her guests a glass of water and a mince pie. They drained their glasses in a trice, but seemed unable to fit the pies into their tiny mouths. They fluttered around the room, picking up objects at random and examining them with child-like curiosity. Finally, they flew out into the garden and entered a hovering orange sphere, still clutching their mince pies. It seemed they had taken quite a shine to Mrs. Hingley's Christmas tree, for the next day it mysteriously vanished. It subsequently reappeared, in pieces, on her lawn – minus its ornaments.

In these times of relative plenty, it is easy to forget that our rural ancestors lived in constant fear of famine. To them, he thought that otherworldly entities might enter their houses to steal or spoil their scarce supply of food would have been deeply unsettling. To the modern mind, however, the idea that aliens might cross our threshold merely to raid our larder seems comically absurd. Consider, for example, the bizarre encounter reported by Indiana teenager Emily Eck in March 1993.

Emily was babysitting a neighbor's toddler one evening when the lights went out and a bright beam shone in from outside. Then a "little purple man" with a "curvy nose" and "big circular ears" walked in through the front door. Ignoring Emily, the little man marched into the kitchen and helped himself to a can of Dr Pepper from the fridge. Then, "as quickly as he had walked in, he walked out." Emily ran to the window just in time to see his flying saucer "take off towards space."

A Ukrainian family reported a similar incident in 1990. Their visitor was a seven-foot-tall silver humanoid with perfect features "like a saint." He materialized in their flat in the middle of the night and headed straight for the fridge, explaining that he wished to take some samples of Earth food. This hardly seems an explanation at all, considering that he could just as easily have materialized in a shop or warehouse and chosen from a far wider range of delicacies.

Equally preposterous was the visit paid by two shining silver beings to Uzbekistani teacher Ruzimat Khayitov in October 1989. The beings entered his flat via the fourth floor balcony and assured him they had no intention of harming him. Then they solemnly poured the contents of his teapot into a container and asked if they might take some cake away with them. Finally, they walked back out on to the balcony and vanished, leaving Khayitov none the wiser as to who they were or where they came from.

**Paying Their Own Way**

On other occasions, otherworldly beings have shown themselves quite capable of buying their own food, albeit not without attracting attention. One such incident occurred in May 1970, when a strange looking couple walked into a St. Louis motel with their two children. The midget-sized adults were scarcely any taller than their offspring, and the entire quartet seemed to be wearing wigs. They had pale faces with prominent dark eyes, slit-like nostrils, and tiny lipless mouths.

"Do you have a room to stay? Do you have a room to stay?" squeaked the male in a falsetto voice. When the desk clerk, Dorothy Simpson, told him how much rooms cost, he looked utterly baffled. After an awkward silence, he pulled out a thick wad of new banknotes and thrust them towards her.

The little man gave his name as "A. Bell." When Simpson asked where he was from, he pointed skywards and trilled, "We come from up there! Up there!" His partner quickly corrected him, saying they were from Hammond, Indiana (although the address she gave proved to be false).

After booking in, the family made their way to the restaurant. The male quizzed the waiter at some length about where vegetables came from before ordering some steak and peas. The others made do with peas and milk. The steak proved an unwise choice, since the little man was unable to open his tiny mouth wide enough to eat it.

Once they had finished eating, the bellhop showed the family to their room. When he switched on the light, the male shouted that it was hurting the children's eyes. The frightened bellhop hastily retreated without waiting for a tip. After that, the strange family was never seen again, even though it should have been impossible for them to leave the building without the desk clerk noticing.

The peculiar character who visited Max's Restaurant in New York in 1967 also had trouble with his steak. According to John Keel, he was "tall and awkward" and "dressed in an ill-fitting black suit that seemed out of style." He had bulging eyes and a sharply pointed chin, and seemed unable to make any sense of the menu. "Food," he mumbled vaguely to the waitress when she asked him what he wanted. When she brought him a steak, he fumbled helplessly with his cutlery and had to be shown how to use it. "Where are you from?" asked the astonished waitress. "Not from here," replied the stranger. "Another world."

Pizza chef Brian Wilson suspected that the unusual couple he served in an Edinburgh takeaway one night in 1990 was also from another world. "They came across as acting as humans, but not doing a very good job of it," he later explained. The two "rather small" and "lopsided" customers introduced themselves by approaching the counter, raising their right hands, and announcing, "Hi! We're Americans!"

"What would you like?" Brian asked them, to which they countered: "What do you make?"

"Pizzas," replied Brian.

"What are pizzas?" asked the Americans.

The couple ordered two cheese and tomato pizzas, and watched Brian intently while he prepared them. The male "kept looking around the shop like he'd never been in a pizza parlor before," while the female pointed at a bowl of green peppers and asked what they were. By now, Brian's colleague Doug had also noticed that there was something rather odd about the couple. The two chefs exchanged glances of disbelief as Brian explained what a pepper was.

"Do they taste nice?" wondered the little woman.

As the pair waited in silence for their pizzas (complete with peppers) to cook, other customers came in and out of the establishment as usual. Once their order was ready, the extraordinary Americans settled their bill and turned to leave. Each took a single bite out of their pizza, then threw the remainder into the garbage can outside the shop.

An equally bizarre customer visited a Ukrainian bakery in October 1989. According to Valentina Stanislavhuk, who served him, he was less than five feet tall, with very pale skin and bright red hair. He wore an ill-fitting green jacket and walked into the shop gabbling in an unrecognizable language. Then he switched to Russian and remarked, "Look at all the bread you have! It will soon disappear." For some reason, Stanislavhuk found this seemingly innocuous comment quite terrifying. She later heard that the little man had made purchases at several other local shops.

Sometimes, rather than taking food, the visitors provide it. But these are cases of *caveat cenator* – eater beware.

**Restaurants of the Gods**

The sharing of food and drink has long played a central role in both sacred and secular customs. Even today, treaties between countries or corporations are invariably accompanied by copious amounts of feasting in the name of diplomacy. Breaking bread with your former enemies remains the most potently symbolic way of welcoming them into the fold. However, when it comes to sharing food with otherworldly beings, tradition dictates that the commerce should be strictly one-way. While mortals were expected to make offerings of food to the gentry, it was considered extremely foolish to accept food *from* them.

As W. Evans Wentz explained: "Human food is what keeps life going in a human body; fairy food is what keeps life going in a fairy body; and since what a man eats makes him what he is physically, so eating the food of Fairyland or of the land of the dead will make the eater partake of the bodily nature of the beings it nourishes. Hence when a man or woman has once entered into such relation or communion with the Otherworld of the dead, or of fairies, by eating their food, his or her physical body by a subtle transformation adjusts itself to the new kind of nourishment, and becomes spiritual like a spirit's or fairy's body, so that the eater cannot re-enter the world of the living."

Unfortunately, it is not always obvious that you *have* "entered into communion" with the Otherworld. Spaniard Julio Fernandez, for example, had no inkling that he had crossed the border between this world and the next when he pulled into a roadside café early one morning in February 1978 and ordered a cup of coffee. He did, however, find it rather strange that the café smelt strongly of pine and that the waiter who served him was wearing rubber gloves and what looked like a blonde wig.

After downing his coffee, Fernandez resumed his journey, only to find himself losing control of his car. It veered off the main road and headed down a dirt trail, where a party of large-headed humanoids was lying in wait. They escorted him on board their craft and gave him a thorough physical examination, revealing only that they came from a place they called "three seven squared." Investigators later discovered that the café Fernandez thought he had visited was actually closed at that hour of the morning – and besides, none of its employees resembled the strange bewigged waiter who had served him.

Civil engineer Tony Clark was similarly unaware that he had left the everyday world behind when he stopped at a roadside café near Manjil, Teheran one hot afternoon in the mid 1950s. The proprietor, Mr. Hovanessian, spoke perfect English and served Clark and his workmate one of the best lunches they had ever tasted. When Clark drove back the same way three months later, he decided to eat at the same cafe. Unfortunately, it no longer existed. Indeed, according to the locals it had *never* existed, and there was no such person as Mr. Hovanessian.

Perhaps the best-known case of a human sharing food with otherworldly beings is that of Joe Simonton. Simonton, a Wisconsin chicken farmer, was eating breakfast one April morning in 1961 when he heard a strange rumbling sound "like knobby tires on a wet pavement." Stepping outside to investigate, he found a flying saucer shaped "like two washbowls turned face to face" hovering in his backyard. Inside stood three brown-skinned figures in knitted uniforms "resembling Italians."

One of the "Italians" came to an open hatchway and held out an empty silver jug while pantomiming the act of drinking. Simonton obligingly filled the jug with water and handed it back. In return, he received the gift of four small pancakes. Disregarding the taboo against consuming fairy food, Simonton ate one. It tasted, he told investigators, rather like cardboard. Another of the pancakes was analyzed by the U.S. Department of Health, who concluded that it was "an ordinary pancake of terrestrial origin." Ufologist Jacques Vallee, however, thought it significant that the pancake lacked salt – a substance that the fairy folk were highly averse to. (One of W. Evans Wentz's informants recalled that "people of miserly nature used to put salt around a cow to keep the pixies away, and then the pixies would lead such mean people astray the very first opportunity that came.")

The prohibition on salt obviously did not apply to the strange visitor who called upon one of John Keel's "silent contactees" in 1967. The witness had just noticed a mysterious silver disc hovering outside her home when the doorbell rang. She found a short Asiatic-looking woman wearing a shimmering dress standing on the doorstep.

"Could I have some salt?" asked the stranger. "I must take a pill."

When given a box of salt, the visitor gulped down a handful then walked away into a clump of bushes. Moments later, the silver disc rose up and sped into the distance. Round about the same time, Keel tells us, "Another contactee was involved in a game which required her to buy large quantities of salt, transport it to Mount Misery, and leave it in a field for the space people in the belief that salt was an essential part of their diet."

## Just Desserts

It should go without saying that advanced extraterrestrial civilizations are unlikely to traverse the vast depths of space simply to borrow salt or sample our pizzas. Even if alien travelers really *are* visiting our planet, the majority of narratives constructed around UFO visions clearly do not concern them. Rather, they are space age myths, which mirror our society just as the rustic folklore of our ancestors mirrored theirs. So, what do these new fantasies tell us about ourselves? Amidst the chaos of high strangeness and paranoia, only one thing seems clear. Our loss of connection with nature has obviously had dire consequences for our mythologies.

An Otherworld located beyond the stars is fundamentally different from one located beneath the nearest hill. UFO mythology lacks both the consistency and the sense of order found in earlier folklore. Fairies may have seemed frightening, sinister beings, but they were nevertheless part of the natural order of things. They could be placated with offerings or combated with natural magic. They feared salt, iron, and churches. Like the devil, they were permitted only a certain amount of power over mortals.

Aliens, on the other hand, are deeply unnatural beings. They originate from outside both Man's kingdom and God's. Despite the best efforts of the contactees and channelers to shoehorn them into existing Theosophical/Christian belief systems, they remain remote and unknowable. They cannot be placated or outwitted. And when they attempt to mould their patterns of behavior to imitate earlier archetypes, they succeed only in making themselves ridiculous. It is one thing for fairies to bake pancakes, but quite another for

UFOnauts to do so. Goblins may steal milk and retain their dignity, but silver-suited humanoids who empty teapots are patently absurd.

If our mythologies have become infected with high strangeness, it can only be because our everyday world has become so bewilderingly strange. If our Otherworld seems so remote and distant, it can only be because we have become so remote and distant from each other. And if our gods now seem quite insane, it can only be because we made them so.

**Sources:**
Peter Brookesmith, *UFO: The Complete Sightings,* Blitz Editions.
Jerome Clark, *Extraordinary Encounters*, ABC-CLIO Ltd.
Mike Dash, *Borderlands*, Heinemann.
Timothy Good, *Unearthly Disclosure*, Arrow Books.
Ron Halliday, *UFO Scotland*, Black & White Publishing.
John Keel, *The Mothman Prophecies*, Hodder & Stoughton.
Robert Kirk, *The Secret Commonwealth of Elves, Fauns & Fairies*, New York Review.
Jenny Randles, *Alien Contact: The First Fifty Years*, Collins & Brown.
Alfred Rosales, Humanoid Database <www.ufoinfo.com/humanoid/index.shtml>
W. Evans Wentz, *The Fairy Faith in Celtic Counties*, Dover Publications.

**CLIFF WILLETT** lives in Norwich, England, where he keeps rats and occasionally works in offices. He plays the piano rather well and the violin rather badly. His other interests include UFOs, Celtic folklore, Jazz and Godzilla. He also contributes to the Fortean blog *Damn Data*. This is his first published article.

# BIOANOMALISTICS:
## A PROPOSAL
### By David Hricenak

In 1973 anthropologist Roger Wescott coined the term anomalistics to cover the study of all phenomena that don't fit into the current scientific paradigm. Of course, many of these phenomena were already being studied by Forteans and referred to as Fortean phenomena. Today the two words are used more or less interchangeably and it seems reasonable that people fascinated by anomalies involving natural history might be referred to as either bioforteans or bioanomalists. But given the choice, in the spirit of Roger Wescott I propose "bioanomalistics" as a semiformal name for this field of study.

So what do bioanomalists study? I would say any alleged phenomenon involving animals, plants, or other organisms would be of interest. I realize that humans are also living organisms but since almost all reported anomalies involve humans in some way I think the field should distinguish itself by mostly focusing on nonhuman life. Still, there is a lot of overlap with practically every other branch of anomalistics including the big three of cryptozoology, UFOlogy, and parapsychology.

The cryptozoology connection is obvious, of course. In fact cryptozoology could be considered a specialized field of bioanomalistics. Cryptozoologists look for evidence of unknown animal species by studying eyewitness accounts and analyzing folk traditions. Bioanomalists use the same sources but we are interested in a wider range of unrecorded biological phenomena.

UFOs have many reported biological effects – think of crop circles and cattle mutilations – and it has been seriously proposed that at least some UFOs may actually be living organisms. (Speaking of crop circles and mutilations, one question for bioanomalists to explore is why both phenomena seem to exclusively target domestic species. I could be wrong, but except for the "saucer nests" reported in the 1960s, I have never heard of a circle formation involving wild vegetation, nor am I aware of a wild animal being mysteriously mutilated.) Also a little biological training can suggest explanations that might not occur to investigators with backgrounds in physical science and engineering. Some UFO sightings have turned out to be birds, insect swarms, and even floating seeds.

Of course this can be carried too far. Skeptic Joe Nickell seems determined to prove that every unexplained entity reported in the last 50 years was actually an owl. Nickell has brought up this idea in *Skeptical Enquirer* articles on the 1955 Kelly-Hopkinsville encounter, the 1952 Flatwoods monster, and the infamous Mothman. In my humble opinion all of these identifications depend on what I like to call the "Yokel Factor," the idea that rural people are uneducated, superstitious, and ignorant of local fauna. Actually a rural Southerner in the 1950s and 1960s would probably have seen and shot many an owl. But that's just my opinion and I'll get off the soapbox. For now.

Finally, while most parapsychologists study people, entire books have been written about the paranormal abilities of plants and animals. What complicates things here is how to distinguish "real" paranormal abilities from little understood but "normal" senses. For example, the often reported ability of various animal species to sense earthquakes probably isn't paranormal, but the many reports of lost pets tracking their owners over hundreds of miles are harder to explain. Also, as with UFOs, biology may sometimes help shed some light on supposedly supernatural phenomena. But again sometimes the explanations seem harder to believe than the supposed phenomena, as in a 1995 *New Scientist* article suggesting that ghost sightings happen when people inhale psychoactive fungal spores.

I would like to flesh out the notion of bioanomalistics as a separate field of study by discussing a few more examples of the phenomena that might fall under its purview and how they might be classified. (For a much more detailed classification system, I would recommend the biology volumes of William Corliss's Sourcebook Project.) One major category of interest would be organisms found in unexpected places. Examples would include various out-of-place animals like big cats in England and Australia, and the old reports of toads found inside solid rock.

In his book *A Cabinet of Medical Curiosities* author Jan Bondeson devotes a chapter to an even less likely phenomenon he calls the Bosom Serpent. I don't know of any modern examples outside of *The Weekly World News,* but it was apparently once a very common belief that snakes and other reptiles could live quite happily in the human stomach. Supposedly they either crawled into a sleeper's open mouth or were swallowed as eggs. Bondeson, a medical doctor, believes these stories may have started when someone vomited up a parasitic worm. Granted some roundworms and tapeworms can be alarmingly big, and the ingested egg explanation is pretty close to how they actually spread. But some of the stories describe something with legs, resembling a lizard or salamander. I don't know of any parasite that looks like that. But until we get a modern account, with a specimen, I guess we'll never know.

A further, somewhat less common category might be anomalous things found inside organisms themselves or inside biological products like seeds or eggs. The "bosom serpent" could also fit this category, of course, as could all those tabloid stories about snakes inside chicken eggs. There is also a remarkable phenomenon called the coconut pearl. I discovered this one on Wayne's Word, a natural history trivia website run by a retired Palomar College biology professor named Wayne Armstrong. It seems that pearls chemically identical to the kind found in mollusks occasionally turn up in what are known as "blind" or infertile coconuts. Several early naturalists reported on this and there are alleged examples in a number of museums and botanical gardens. But are any genuine? Professor Armstrong doubts it but admirably details all of the pros and cons on his site. The bottom line seems to be don't buy one on Ebay.

Anomalous behavior is another topic of major interest to bioanomalists. Mainstream biologists are reluctant to attribute intelligent or human-like behavior to "lower" animals. This is the sin of anthropomorphism, so such behavior is seldom acknowledged. One example involves those brainy birds, the crows. For centuries there have been reports of crows ganging up on and killing members of their own flocks. Why? Nonbiologists aren't afraid of being called anthropomorphists, of course, but folk interpretations have varied as culture has changed. In a more violent era these incidents were assumed to be trials; the victim had committed some heinous crime, maybe the avian equivalent of stealing a loaf of bread, and was being executed. In the more enlightened 1990s at least one writer thought the dead crows were ill and flock members were performing euthanasia. So far as I know no one has ever autopsied an "executed" bird so who knows what's really going on? The crows, presumably, but they're not telling.

My next example involves both anomalous bird behavior and the anomalous properties of plants. In their book *Secrets of the Soil,* Peter Tompkins and Christopher Bird discuss biologist Albert Schatz's research on those remarkable composite organisms lichens and their contributions to soil production. In the course of this research Schatz came across the writings of explorer Percy Fawcett. In the early twentieth century Fawcett led several expeditions into the Amazon rainforest in search of lost cities and finally disappeared there in 1925. The cryptozoologically inclined may be familiar with his accounts of unknown hominids and giant anacondas. But Fawcett's main interests were archeological and he was fascinated by Inca stonework. As described in pretty much every book on ancient mysteries, the Inca built with multi-ton stone blocks that fit together so well a knife blade can't be inserted between them. Fawcett became convinced that their secret was the ability to soften the stone beforehand.

Fawcett's idea ties in with Schatz's discovery that lichens produce acids that enable them to dissolve stone, acquiring vital minerals and anchoring themselves. But the Inca didn't use lichens. Fawcett collected several anecdotal clues to their stone softening method. One native informant told him of the nest building behavior of a bird called the pito. Apparently this bird pecks nest holes in solid rock, after first softening the stone by rubbing it with the leaves of a certain plant.

Another correspondent, an Englishman, wrote of how his cousin had had his spurs eroded away after walking through a patch of plants with dark red leaves. He was later told that these were the plants the Inca used to soften stone. When Schatz retold this story in his book *Teaching Science With Soil,* he received a letter from a Peruvian priest who claimed to have rediscovered the same plant, known as *harakkeh'ann* in the Quechua language. I don't know what happened after that, but if anyone had taken Schatz seriously some corporation would probably have patented the plant extract by now.

Anomalous behavior often reflects anomalous abilities. There is an African rodent known as the crested rat (*Lophiomys imhausi*), which, when threatened, thrashes its body, snaps its teeth, erects the hair on its back, and releases a foul smelling substance. Naturalist Lyall Watson has witnessed this display and found it anomalously disturbing. He believes that *Lophiomys* may produce a pheromone-like substance that actually affects the fear-inducing area of the brain.

Emotion producing rat secretions are anomalous but don't violate the laws of physics. But some smaller creatures might, at least according to naturalist and anomalist Ivan Sanderson. In a *Fate* magazine article, later reprinted in his 1967 book *Things,* Sanderson discusses his research on the *Atta* or leaf-cutting ants. If you have ever watched a nature documentary on the South American rain forest, you have probably seen these insects marching single file and carrying bits of leaf overhead like parasols. You may even know that they chew the leaves into mulch to grow the fungus that is their only food source.

All of this is amazing enough, but Sanderson also believed that these ants invented teleportation long before Captain Kirk ever beamed up on *Star Trek.* Apparently, the queen ant spends all of her time in a sealed chamber, laying up to 150 million eggs in a lifetime. If she disappears from her chamber, it is usually assumed that she has died and workers have removed the body. But Sanderson claimed that *Atta* queens, marked with dye, have vanished from one chamber and reappeared in another. I have also seen the same claim made about termites, unrelated insects with a similar lifestyle. Not surprisingly I have never seen the subject discussed by mainstream entomologists.

Most anomalies, biological or not, are things that "shouldn't happen" but apparently do. My last example is something that "should" happen but apparently doesn't. Much, maybe too much, has been written about the phenomenon of SHC, spontaneous human combustion. But what I haven't seen addressed is why reports involving nonhuman animals are practically nonexistent. Ivan Sanderson, in a chapter on SHC in his book *Investigating the Unexplained,* claimed to have a number of animal cases on file but never, to my knowledge, published any details. If this isn't just a case of selective reporting, one has to wonder why this controversial phenomenon only affects our species.

Oddly enough there does seem to be some evidence for spontaneous plant combustion. In his book *Remarkable Trees of the World,* Thomas Pakenham states that African baobab trees have been known to combust. This is remarkable for two reasons. First, because baobabs are also known for their ability to hold and store water, and second because Pakenham later wrote an entire book on these trees and never mentioned the subject again.

These are just a few examples of the kind of subjects we bioanomalists are interested in. I could go on and on, but I won't. Let's just say that, like more conventional naturalists, we never have to worry about getting bored or running out of mysteries to investigate.

**DAVID HRICENAK** majored in biology from Wilkes College (now Wilkes University) in Wilkes-Barre PA. He wrote for the *INFO Journal* back the late 1970s and early 1980s and more recently a few nature articles for a local monthly newspaper in Milford, Pennsylvania. He is currently writing and pursuing a teaching career in the Nashville, Tennessee.

# WHISPERS FROM THE EARTH:
## CAN SCIENCE GRASP THE HINTS
## BEFORE AN EARTHQUAKE?
### BY SHARON HILL

Scientists have struggled to understand how earthquakes occur – precisely where, exactly when, and how strong. We know that an earthquake is a movement of the earth's surface caused by the dislocation of the plates that make up the crust or a release of energy from underground stresses. Today, seismologists know far more about earthquake processes than ever before, but still they are unable to predict earthquakes with certainty in workable time frames.

In the 1970s, scientists were optimistic that earthquake prediction was possible through warnings from precursors. They thought that foreshocks occurred in a predictable way and indicated when the main shock was close at hand. They observed that some earthquakes occur when there is a gap in time or space along a fault. Measurements of how fast certain vibration waves passed through the ground seemed to suggest that a predictable change occurs prior to an earthquake. When research showed that these techniques worked sporadically, not nearly all the time as they should, the attitude of seismologists soured on earthquake prediction, especially in the U.S.

An article in the journal *Science* in 1996, entitled "Earthquakes Cannot Be Predicted," punctured the balloon of anyone who thought that earth movements were knowable. The expert consensus was that the faulted areas were so different, with individual stresses and physical conditions, and reacted so uniquely, it was not possible to be successful at wholesale prediction.

Perhaps that conclusion was correct for that moment in time. But, should they have given up? New and innovative ideas about earthquake prediction were developing in other countries like China, Japan and Russia. We can look back to ancient times for the root of these new ideas. Long ago, farmers, peasants, and early naturalists noticed the clues that signaled stress was building deep underground and about to give way.

**Animals gone crazy**

Of all the scientific anomalies that are related to earthquakes and earthquake prediction, none is more curious or mystifying than the heaps of reports of strange animal behavior prior to earthquakes.

Ever since ancient people recorded their thoughts about the shaking earth, they have remarked upon the behavior of their animals. The best-known story comes from Japan, where a huge catfish living under the ground was thought to cause the earth to heave whenever it wiggled. Catfish have been observed to jump and twist violently right before a quake. It is very likely that these observations helped craft the often-repeated myth.

Along with fish, both domestic and wild, a wide variety of animals have been described in anecdotal reports as sensing a coming earthquake. Their actions greatly differ.

Some animals eat more.

Birds change their songs or sounds; they refuse to land or preen their feathers constantly.

Underground animals come to the surface.

Caged or penned animals become highly agitated, aggressive, fearful, or try to escape.

Wild animals will leave their home territory.

Domestic animals, such as cats, will remove their young from buildings, clean themselves frequently, or be especially attentive to their owner, crying or acting nervous.

Dogs notoriously howl or bark and become preoccupied with sniffing the ground.

Insects may suddenly disappear or appear in swarms.

Aquatic animals leave the water or head far out to sea.

Animals may act confused and appear in unlikely areas.

The strange behavior may be exhibited seconds before a quake or up to a month before.

Minutes before Hawaii's 6.7 magnitude quake in October 2006, a local television reporter noticed fish jumping out of a lagoon. Even for a small tremor, estimated at 2.4 magnitude in mid-December 2006 in Sinking Spring, Pennsylvania, locals reported that their dogs were subdued or nervous in the hours before the quake. Also in mid-December 2006, the obituary for Max the pig, beloved pet of actor George Clooney, gave the animal credit for waking George minutes prior to the onset of a California quake years ago. Earth scientists regard such episodes as either coincidences or occasions of selective memory.

In China, changes in animal behavior are officially accepted as a precursor to a quake; the government prints information booklets on the subject to give to the public. In 1974-5, in Haicheng, a strong earthquake was preceded by a long list of animal anomalies that were recorded by the population and the data was fed back to scientists. Along with other precursors, the animal behaviors were credited with helping to predict the quake and save many lives.

With the huge variety of animals reacting to some earthquake signals from the earth, they can't all be responding to the same precursors. Different animals are sensitive to different things.

People are probably the least sensitive animals, as we see, hear, smell, and perceive far less of the natural environment than animals. However, even people occasionally react to earth signs. Data collected before the Kobe, China quake in 1995 revealed reports of children in the fault area who awoke before the quake and people who reported unusual feelings of fatigue, dizziness, or illness.

The American seismology community flatly denies any suggestion of animals as earthquake predictors, however. As reasons, they point to the wide range of behaviors reported, the inability to measure animal behavior, and the frequent lack of animal anomalies before some quakes.

It does seem clear, however, that animals do react to some environmental signal before at least some earthquakes, just as they are aware of some approaching change in the weather. What are the animals reacting to? Can we ever measure what they feel?

Stranger still, we must also include plants as potentially responsive to such earth signals. Records exist of some species growing vigorously, while others bloom early, rebloom or wilt in coordination with large seismic events. Still other plants close their leaves prior to the shaking or tremble in the still air preceding the shock. With roots reaching into the ground, are they detecting signals that we are missing?

### Earth sounds

Howling and whistling noises have been associated with tremors. Explosive, echoing, or rumbling sounds (earthquake sounds) have been reported by local people in quake-prone areas around the world minutes, hours, or days before quakes. These sounds are rare, but where they do occur, they are reported again in quakes that follow. Scientists have not been able to record such sounds, and there is no explanation for what may cause them.

### Paranormal effects

Absent electric light and modern stoves, stories have been told of candle flames bent and distorted without a breeze, as well as hearth fires that did not get hot enough to cook food. There are also reports of corked wine turning cloudy or milk spoiling overnight.

Magnets holding nails suddenly lose their attraction and the nails drop. Iron chains swing without a breeze.

Sometimes evil spirits are credited with these events.

Later, in the days of telegraph wires, signals and static were transmitted out of nowhere. This was a provocative hint that some electrical signal from the earth was being inadvertently detected by human technology.

A ghostly, modern phenomenon, not mentioned in the ancient reports, is the response of electronic devices to unseen signals before a quake. (Ikeya, 2004) Clocks stop or the hands rotate quickly. Appliances suddenly turn on. Cell phones ring without callers. TVs flicker and display distortion. Intercoms buzz. Florescent lamps dim.

Spooky effects such as these may have a more prosaic explanation but scientists have yet to clarify the mechanism.

### Water

Water levels, in wells and on the surface, have commonly been noted to drop suddenly prior to a quake. Groundwater levels in Pennsylvania were affected subtly, but noticeably, by the Alaska earthquakes of 1964 and 2002, and in Virginia water levels jumped then dropped in response to the giant 2005 Asian quake that spawned the deadly tsunami, so we know that the mechanisms are widespread as a result of the quake.

Groundwater can also become cloudy or muddy and may change in taste or odor. The sea may become still as glass. Ponds may become murky.

**Earthquake weather**

If you live in an area prone to earthquakes, you might have heard stories about earthquake weather. Earthquake weather is said to be a dry, hot, oppressive calmness. It leaves one with the miserable feeling that something bad is about to occur. People feel weak, nauseous, and uneasy. There are also reports of the atmosphere becoming dark or "thick" with smoke, dust, fog, or vapors.

Thunderstorms have been associated with earthquakes.

Just prior to or after a quake, the moon or sun may appear red, surrounded by a halo, or elongated in shape. The stars may appear closer. Short-arc vertical or horizontal rainbows have been seen. Early observers, like Aristotle, noted these unusual weather characteristics. (Tributsch, 1982)

There are numerous instances of bizarre-shaped clouds (earthquake clouds or EQCs) appearing in the sky days before an earthquake. Prior to the 1995 quake in Kobe, Japan, several such clouds were captured in photographs. Proverbs tell of dragon or snake-like clouds foretelling the coming of an earthquake. A large cloud also appeared suddenly in a blue sky moments before a quake in Tokyo, Japan in 1923. (Ikeya, 2004)

EQCs are stationary and do not drift away like normal clouds. Diffuse, low clouds can settle into an earthquake fog. Earthquake fogs have been described in historic documents. The association between fogs and clouds and strong tremors is such that it was once thought that they were the cause of the quakes that followed soon after. Aristotle forged a link between earthquakes and atmospheric conditions that lasted until the Middle Ages. There are historic and current reports of the "breath of the earth" having a sulfuric odor or the smell of decay.

Mainstream science does not correlate atmospheric changes with seismic activity and does not consider these as precursors to a coming quake.

**Glows, balls and curtains of lights**

Gaining more credibility as earthquake precursors are the various luminous phenomena that occur before or during a strong quake. The high quality evidence for these events comes from historical writings and photographs, especially from Japan where earthquakes are so very common.

Earthquake lights (EQLs) come in a great variety of shapes and colors and can appear out of the ground or from the sky. They can be seen moments before a quake as a glowing dome above the ground or as flashes, curtains, sheets, funnels, arcs, or balls that may even travel along the fault line in blue, red, green, yellow, orange, purple or white.

Dozens of good photographs helped bring EQLs out of folklore and into the realm of scientific investigation. However, there is still no good explanation available, mainly because there does not exist a way to objectively measure these lights.

A strange account of balls of lights comes from fishermen in Turkey before a 1999 quake. They described fireballs (ball lightning?) in the sky and undersea explosions with bright balloons of light ascending through the water. Their fishing nets were burned by the fireballs. (Ikeya, 2004)

Modern science rejects such reports, however. Without data collected in an objective way, the idea of EQLs cannot be seriously evaluated.

**What is happening?**

Unusual animal behavior, anomalous atmospherics, light displays, sounds, spooky happenings around the house: is the earth sending signals to which we fail to listen? They have not been diligently recorded or studied.

The primary question is: "Are these things really happening as people have described?" Can they be cases of mistaken observations, observations after the fact (where we attribute every little thing as associated with the quake), or hoaxes? This basic question must be asked in any circumstance involving an eyewitness; human observation and memory are notoriously unreliable.

Precursors of earthquakes have been reported since ancient times and the phenomena are still being experienced today. In modern times, there are instances where a multitude of reliable observers have documented these events, even by camera, videotape, and sensors.

Thus, the reports have entered the field of mainstream science. Though few scientists are willing to study them, there has been some progress towards understanding these phenomena. For example, M. Ikeya has determined that there is sufficient correlation between the time and location of the reported phenomena, which shows that the events are definitively related to the subsequent quake and are not just coincidental.

But how does one go about studying these events? We can't predict earthquakes so how can we be prepared to study precursors? On a more basic level, how can governmental and university scientists obtain funding to study phenomena that many of their colleagues discount? Scientists who go against the grain often suffer some professional discredit, even when their experiments produce positive results. (Ikeya, 2004; Tributsch, 1982)

A theory must be developed to account for the invisible source that causes these observations. Among the several "invisible" sources that may explain these observations are gases, charged particles (ions), electrical fields, magnetic fields, infra- or ultrasound, infrared or ultraviolet light. People can rarely detect these without the use of specialized equipment. However, a source that is basically undetectable to an average person may be detectable to animals or sensitive electronic devices, or may interact with the environment in such a way as to become noticeable to some people.

Several theories have been proposed to explain the above ground phenomena that occur in conjunction with below-the-ground activity. Newer hypotheses suggest that the earth often tells us well in advance that she is about to heave.

Let's examine what happens prior to an earthquake. Rock is being strained, compressed, heated, and bent down to the scale of its component mineral crystals, before it finally breaks *en masse*. Before the rock mass breaks and unzips, it cracks. Tiny cracks form in the rock structure. The stress and strain placed on rock in an active fault zone changes the intrinsic properties of the rock. Can we measure the change? And, if we can measure it, can we use it to predict when and where the quake will happen?

Centuries of scientific and popular observations has given us a body of anecdotes peppered with actual physical measurements and recordings of anomalous phenomena occurring prior to large earthquakes. This fact is not in doubt. The failure of these signals to become a practical means by which we predict earthquakes in the short term results from (1) the unreliability of the phenomena, (2) the irreproducibility of the phenomena, and (3) an inadequate explanation for the phenomena (which follows from the first two). We might add that there is a hesitation to divert from the known path in science, but that excuse is invalid. In terms of earthquake prediction, the time may be now to diverge from the path.

When we consider anomalous earthquake-related phenomena (AERP), we don't get far by just collecting the stories unless we proceed to analyze, interpret, and explain them. Then, to be of future value, they must be used to predict.

### Release of gases and ions

As discussed, squeezing, stretching, and (micro)fracturing of the rock is inherent in the faulted area. Many AERP appear to have an electrical explanation – one that's related to charged particles, currents and voltage.

An obvious consequence of stress and friction is heat. Reports of hot, sticky weather preceding a quake suggests that fault zones give off heat. Surface temperature recordings have indicated a rise prior to a seismic event. (Pulinets & Boyarchuk, 2004) Then, in 2006, Indian scientists reported that a bloom of plankton offshore prior to a quake may be the result of a release of thermal energy that caused the local sea temperature to rise.

It is well known that gases escape from the ground before and during an earthquake. Water vapor, methane, and other gases resulting from decomposing organic material may be released. Near the epicenter of the 1995 Kobe quake, a mineral water bottling plant noted that the gas content in the water varied prior to the earthquake. In Iceland, a similar observation was noted in 2002 when chemical constituents of a hot spring increased enormously within a ten-week span prior to a 5.8 magnitude quake. Gas release may serve to explain the (nonelectrical) reports of putrid smells or atmospheric lens effects that leads to observations of an elongated sun or moon before a quake.

Radon, a common radioactive gas trapped within rock, is released when the rock forms tiny cracks (microfractures). Increased radon in the air and groundwater has been measured numerous times prior to earthquakes.

Due to its radioactivity, radon can ionize air. Animals and people respond to ionized air. Positively charged ions in the air may affect serotonin levels. Serotonin is a hormone that regulates several physiological aspects in humans, such as mood, appetite, and whether one feels well or unwell.

Ionization of the air (by radon or other means) can create particles known as aerosols. Ions are electrically charged and serve as nuclei for condensation. Aerosol particles can carry soot, dust, droplets, crystals (especially salt), pollen, even virus and bacteria. The formation and accumulation of aerosols generated by underground processes would vary depending on the current weather conditions, the geology of the rock, and other aerosols in the air. For example, wind and rain will quickly dissipate the particles. Aerosols may only last a few minutes after which they decay. However, if the mechanism that is creating them persists, a new supply can continually be formed.

The aerosol hypothesis, put forth by H. Tributsch as an explanation for various AERP, posits that a coming quake influences the near-surface atmosphere to such a degree that unusual meteorological events occur.

There have been reports of metals in gaseous form being expelled in tectonically active areas. These metallic aerosols may play a role in the mechanisms that relate seismic activity to anomalies in the upper reaches of the atmosphere (a theory called "lithospheric-ionospheric [or seismo-ionospheric] coupling"). Release of gases may be a crucial, first step in a complicated process. (Pulinets & Boyarchuk, 2004)

## Generating electricity

The idea of earth currents was discussed in 1890 by John Milne, who is known as the "father of seismology." There are other examples of natural electrical phenomena from the earth other than lightning bolts. Glowing patches on mountains have been observed as the electricity is dissipated into the sky across a broad area. St. Elmo's fire has been observed on the high masts of boats; it even occurs on high pointed structures on land with enough regularity for it to have been studied. Earthquake lights may be in the same category as anomalous ball lightning, flickering ground lights (known as "spooklights"), and perhaps even some reports of UFOs in that they can manifest from static electricity generated from the ground surface. An intense electrical field and electromagnetic pulses generated at a fault zone can potentially explain the various AERP discussed here. Dr. Michael Persinger proposed the tectonic strain theory in 1975 relating light phenomena at fault zones to what eyewitnesses report as UFOs.

Rock can actually produce electricity due to the "piezometric" effect. It is the result of the ability of crystals, especially quartz, to generate a voltage in response to applied stress. The act of squeezing a quartz crystal induces a polarity in the crystal (one end positive, the other negative). This allows a current to travel across the crystal. Piezoelectricity can free up electrical charges. These escaped charges (ions) may contribute to the generation of a strong electrical field above the ground surface or aerosols. Quartz is abundant in the earth's crust, especially in granite, the common foundation rock for continents. Curiously, in an assessment of areas with and without defined precursors, those zones with quartz-poor rock, such as New Zealand, appear to have fewer observable AERP. (Ikeya, 2004)

Light can result when bonds are broken in a crystal when it is rubbed or cracked. This is called triboluminescence. The broken bond creates a positive and negative charge that recombine as a spark. This can easily be demonstrated by cracking a LifeSaver candy in a dark room. It has also been observed while cutting diamonds. Scientists are still far from understanding this effect since some substances exhibit this property while others do not. It is unknown if this phenomenon is occurring in fault zones.

If enormous electrical currents are being generated, through known or as yet unknown mechanisms, they may potentially serve as the signal we can measure to predict quakes. Also, these mechanisms may result in observable surface manifestations (AERP). It might be a cascading effect, beginning with the rock fracturing at microscopic scale, where the buildup of stress in the rock generates electrical energy that can result in a release of light and measurable electricity. Different types of EQLs could be a result of the difference in charge distribution and the uneven field across adjacent areas.

A stream of charged particles is called plasma. Examples of plasmas are lightning bolts or candle flames. What observers see as various forms of EQLs may be, in fact, plasmas, a stream of electrons from the ground generating visible light.

Laboratory experiments where crystalline rock samples are subjected to high pressure show that the electrical resistance of water-saturated rock changes just before it shatters. Experiments show that the intensity of the electric field generated is greater through the process of microfracturing the rock than it is at the actual breakage. (Bolt, 1993)

Some researchers have abandoned the piezoelectricity theory as a cause of earthquake precursor phenomena. It is hard to accept that the rocks can become conductive enough to generate an electrical pulse. The assumption made is that the random orientation of crystals in the rock would not allow for the effect to propagate and that the generated positive and negative charges would simply cancel each other out. However, lab experiments have shown that if at least some of the crystals are oriented in the same direction, voltages can occur in rocks under stress. Even if only one percent of the quartz grains are aligned, considerable voltage can be produced. (Ikeya, 2004)

If it is feasible for electrical conditions to occur, the movement of charge through rock will generate electromagnetic waves.

**Electricity and magnetism**

Electricity is related to magnetism. The passing of current generates electromagnetic waves. Prior to strong earthquakes in fair weather, scientists have observed anomalous electrical fields and electromagnetic pulses from ULF to VHF. Electromagnetic pulses can travel through the ground, air, and water. Intense electric fields formed by the microfracturing of the underground rock would extend above the ground surface. But there will be regions on earth where the tectonic action is so deep that the EM waves won't reach the surface and no precursors would occur.

We are exposed to weak electromagnetic fields all the time. Many experiments have shown that they generally don't affect us. Animals experience small but unimpressive magnetic field changes periodically and rarely act unusually. The change in magnetic field can influence some animals, but the field is constantly changing especially during solar wind storms. The change in the field appears to be relatively minor as a result of seismic activity compared to these background-level influences.

Long wave electromagnetic radiation appears whenever electrical charges are generated or neutralized. Electric charge and electromagnetic signals are not detected by seismographs because there is no vibration, whereas a radio receiver is a good detector of electromagnetic waves. AM bands on a radio will transmit the EM noise generated from nearby thunderstorms (where lightning provides the discharge of electricity). Radio interference has been mentioned as a possible precursor to quakes.

A bent candle flame, or a candle that is hard to light or burns inefficiently, has been noted as an AERP. Fire is a plasma. Ikeya reproduced the anomalous effect by generating a charge on the ground that attracts the flame. He has reproduced many other precursor phenomena in the lab by exploring the effects of electrical fields and EM waves. He now has very good evidence to suggest that these conditions are occurring as part of the earthquake's progress, and he has shown that the values that nature could produce may be sufficient to show such effects.

One explanation for AERP we might discount is a change in the earth's magnetic field before an earthquake. It appears that the change is so small, it is negligible. There is a story of a magnet that hung on a wall in a building in Tokyo. In 1855, nails held by the magnet suddenly fell as if the magnet had lost its power. It may seem that the magnetic field was disturbed, but the electrical charge from the ground may well have overwhelmed the magnet's strength, causing the nails to sway and be attracted to the ground.

**Disturbance in the upper atmosphere**

If we assume these mechanisms are at work in the stressed rock, large electrical fields can occur hours, days, or even more than a month before the seismic release. The seismo-ionospheric theory, in development by Russian scientists for decades, suggests these fields extend so high above the earth's surface that they can affect the upper reaches of the atmosphere and interact with the earth's global electrical circuit. This area of the atmosphere, 50-1000 kilometers above the surface where the interaction is seen, is called the ionosphere. Soviet military satellites have recorded changes in the ionosphere in the days before a large quake.

The ionosphere is said to start to "feel" the zone of pending seismic activity from the preparatory mechanisms of a magnitude 5 event and above. (Pulinets & Boyarchuk, 2004) U.S. scientists have not caught on to such foreign ideas but more experimentation and modeling has produced a viable theory that is being tested; they feel that the physical mechanisms must be studied and understood first before any promise of prediction can be examined.

Low altitude satellites have recorded seismo-electromagnetic waves over earthquake-prone areas such as Armenia. The ionosphere disturbances over other seismically active locations have also been recorded. Curiously, the generation of these charges on the ground may not necessarily mean that a massive fracturing of the rock (an earthquake) will occur there. It can instead indicate that the fault movement is blocked. Thus, we can only say that electromagnetic phenomena can indicate rock fracturing with a possible earthquake to follow.

**Can we explain EQLs?**

Until recently, most scientists rejected the reality of earthquake lights because there was not a satisfactory means to account for their origin. The lights do not serve as dependable alarm signals before a quake but are contingent upon whether the required large electrical energy has built up. This can only happen when the subsequent quake is large. Lights appear to be evidence that an electrostatic charge is present.

According to calculations by Ikeya, the shape of the glow produced by an intense electrical field generated via underground fracturing would be a dome or ball shape. The concentration of air ions need not be as great to produce animal behavior anomalies.

## Can we explain earthquake sounds?

Stress and local fracturing in massive rock may generate earthquake sounds. An example of this sound-stress phenomenon occurs when one is near a metal or wood structure on a hot, sunny day. As the material warms or cools rapidly, the change in temperature results in stress in the material that gives a noticeable "crack" on occasion. The material is not visibly damaged but the internal stress of expansion or shrinkage is released. Ultrasound and infrasound might result from rock cracking. These frequencies might be out of the range of hearing for the average person but not those sensitive to such frequencies. Some animals may be sensitive to them as well. But sound as a precursor is not very reliable since it can be swamped by background noise or dampened within the rock.

## Can we explain earthquake weather?

The release of gases, the formation of aerosols, and the electrified air might all play a part in the formation of anomalous clouds and fogs reported as part of "earthquake weather." The ionization of air can explain the feeling of hot oppressiveness that hangs over the land. It is unclear if the thermal energy released at a fault contributes to the phenomenon. It is clear that no particular type of weather *causes* earthquakes, but there may be circumstances in which factors combine to signal changes happening in the earth below.

## Can we explain anomalous animal behavior?

Animal reactions are most likely the result of a combination of several factors. Not all animals are sensitive to the same environmental stimuli. Some are acutely sensitive to smell (dogs) and others are not (birds). Some can sense vibrations but others, such as domestic animals, are surrounded by vibrations and noise that cancel out subtle signals.

Animals can be very sensitive to electric fields. Some have organs specifically for navigating or catching prey using electrical signals. Sharks and catfish, in particular, have extraordinarily sensitive electrosensory systems, which they use to capture hidden prey and for communication, orientation, and navigation. Mammals have hair that acts as a sensor for electrical fields. (Humans can feel the prickly sensation and watch hair rise in response to static electricity.) Feathers, whiskers, and antennae can receive electrical signals from the environment.

An electric field induces current to flow in the body. Animals, plants, objects and atmosphere may all be responding to the seismo-electromagnetic signals from the epicentral area of the coming quake, which is called the "earthquake preparation area." The generated electrical fields are strong enough for local discharges to generate high frequency EM waves. A great number of results reveal background anomalies in EM emission levels right up to the moment of the quake; they may even continue after the quake. These signals have been recorded by individuals who had no intention of correlating them to earthquakes.

Animals also have been reported to act unusually before and during other catastrophes like storms, tsunami landfalls, and house fires. Crocodiles in Japan were said to behave violently prior to an earthquake in the area and had displayed similar behavior prior to approaching storms, which may indicate they are responding to EM waves. (Ikeya, 2004) Because we see parallels in behavior between coming storms and earthquakes, perhaps the underlying reason is also the same. Some animals probably respond through surface contact while others seem to perceive it through the air. Ikeya's experiments showed that animals expressed distress when the applied voltage was effectively too low to actually hurt them.

His experiments reproduced the reported behavior of animals before earthquakes by using generated EM waves. However, it does appear to depend on the particular species and individual sensitivity – animals like mice, rats, and parrots showed odd behavior at low currents. Different animals attempted to move away from an electrical field; tried to minimize the effect by avoiding water, rubbing or preening themselves in an attempt to relieve irritation; or minimized contact with the ground, stayed in contact with metal, or aligned their body with or against the field. To produce a response, Ikeya noted that the earthquake must be greater than M4, the animal must be within 30 km of the epicenter and the intensity of the field must be greater than 1 volt/minute. The mechanism by which animals respond to EM waves is not clear.

If we consider the process of the rock fracturing on a small scale prior to breaking at the large scale and giving way to the quake and creating EM pulses, then compression of rock in laboratory experiments should produce the desired effect as well. In fact, animal experiments have shown that mice become restless and show signs of fear and distress when in proximity to rock under pressure prior to bursting. Anecdotal evidence also exists suggesting that animals sense rockslides and mine rock failures and move away from the affected area well before the event.

Animal behavior experiments show that the electrical field values and their effects are consistent with those generated in a seismic event. Ikeya posits that local stress changes in rock generate charges via the piezometric effect during microfracturing, frictional electricity, or fluid flow electrokinetics. As an electric dipole collapses, it produces EM waves in pulses, which causes animals to respond physiologically. By using results on the tolerances of animals to electrical effects, he estimated the electrical field strength needed to produce such effects. A large earthquake, producing six billion watts (a small fraction of the overall potential), can theoretically produce these effects.

### The evidence suggests...

While many questions remain, experimental results have shown that earthquake-related anomalies might be reproducible in a lab and a reasonable theory can be postulated to account for them. In summary, those anomalous atmospheric changes can be accounted for if the electrical effects resulting from stressed rock conditions are occurring. There may also be some unknown mechanism at work underground that scientists have not yet measured or accounted for. Above all, it must be understood that each earthquake is slightly different and behaves in a unique way. Precursory activity involves multiple factors in the chain of events and is just as unique.

## State of prediction

It wasn't until 1800 or so that theories about the causes of earthquakes mentioned the idea of precursors. Precursors, such as water level changes, were just "curiosities of nature." In the early 1900s, an instrument called a "coherer" was used in Italy to detect electromagnetic emissions, probably the first attempt to produce a practical device to recognize precursors before a quake. (Martinelli, 1998)

Decades ago, the theory of rock dilatancy prior to a quake was tested. Dilatancy occurs when the rock develops cracks (or "dilates") due to stress. This process might be measured by observing a lowered velocity of artificially (or naturally) generated seismic waves, ground uplift or tilt, increased radon emission, and a lowering of electrical resistivity through the rock. After the initial dilatancy, which increases the volume of the rock, there was presumed to be an influx of water into the fault zone. Consequently, the seismic pressure wave speed would return to normal, the electrical resistivity would continue to decrease, and there would be an increase in the number of small local quakes just before the fault ruptured. Employing this theory for prediction produced less than stellar results and it was more or less abandoned, though not invalidated, as seismologists pursued the idea of foreshocks to predict the main shock. (Pulinets & Boyarchuk, 2004; Ikeya, 2004; Bolt, 1993)

In 2004, a controversial forecasting theory, proposed by V. Kellis-Borok and based on past earthquakes patterns and statistics, failed to be the hoped for breakthrough, but it brought the conundrum of prediction back to the attention of the community of seismologists. (Cyranoski, 2004)

In the last 20 years, the study of changes in electrical fields before earthquakes has made some progress. First begun in Greece, Japan, and France, this approach left American seismologists skeptical. But the results were valid. Changes prior to earthquakes have been measured, and electromagnetic anomalies have been documented. But it is still not clear how the measured anomalies are linked with the quake itself, what they mean, and how they can be potentially used as a predictive tool.

There are difficulties in measuring electromagnetic changes

associated with earthquakes because of the presence of other wave sources such as lightning, magnetic storms, and artifacts from our cultural machinery. To eliminate the noise, the best locations to monitor appear to be deep boreholes or the sea floor, neither of which are very practical. There are regular variations (hourly, daily, seasonally) in addition to a noisy background from storms, precipitation, winds, dust, etc. These factors complicate the processing of data to determine if a seismic-generated signal is buried within it.

Radon monitoring is being used to look for a characteristic increase and decrease just before a quake. Observation of water levels is inexpensive and easy to measure, but it gives us little information as to when and where the quake might occur.

During the 1974-1975 lead up to the Haicheng, China quake, along with the strange animal behavior observed by everyday folk, ground indicators suggested that a quake was about to occur and prompted the government to act. A 7.3 magnitude earthquake then destroyed half the buildings around the epicenter, but there were few human victims thanks to the advance warning. This was considered a success but, unfortunately, animals don't always react reliably before a quake. Their behavior is not consistently recognizable as odd or indicative of a coming quake. There may be several alternate reasons why animals behave differently than normal. Therefore, animal behavior isn't the best gage to use to predict quakes. In addition, animal observations are more difficult today because animals are not as integral to our lives as they once were when they often worked along side us and were part of our livelihood. Our technological and busy society has lost some of its ability to gain from observing nature. Now, we rely on other people or electronics to tell us the condition of the environment.

Satellites have provided us with unique views of our world. Remote sensing equipment that measures changes in the ionosphere is proving to be a worthwhile tool to help judge where the next epicenter will be. Ionospheric precursors give a quite reasonable and useful expectation time of one-to-five days. A statistical study done by Chen in 1999 showed that ionospheric precursors occurr within five days of a magnitude 5 event 73 percent of the time, but 100 percent of the time for magnitude 6 quakes. The one-to-five-day interval is now well established for ionospheric anomalies. There are complex electrodynamical, meteorological, and chemical processes involved in producing an ionospheric disturbance. However, satellite studies have clearly been able to indicate the region of the future quake. (Pulinets & Boyarchuk, 2004)

### A new science

An earthquake of magnitude 5.7 occurred near Coyote Lake, California, in August 1979. The area was crammed with geophysical instruments to measure tectonic strain. Not a single precursor was identified with these instruments. However, the local spring experienced a change in water level and some abnormal animal behavior was reported. The Parkfield experiment to capture an expected earthquake finally culminated in 2004 with no obvious precursors, and ever since then hopes for prediction science has waned. What are the precise conditions under which an earthquake preparation area exhibits precursory activity? Not only are these conditions unknown, but the actual occurrence of precursors is still widely doubted by seismologists.

If charged particles are indeed released from the ground prior to a large quake, prediction may be possible by measuring the release of gases, positive ions near the ground surface, changes in the atmospheric electrical fields above the fault area, changes in the vertical stream of ions into the atmosphere, an increase in EM radiation, the appearance of electrical earth currents, or changes in the electrical potential of groundwater or surface waters. But what and how to measure must still be decided.

Much has been learned about earth signals before a quake. The most important may be the electrical effect. Ikeya hopes that recent progress will spawn a new discipline called "electromagnetic seismology." The most interesting aspect is how wide-ranging the effect may be. It was previously assumed that any changes in the ionosphere were caused by environmental variability, geomagnetic storms, and the like. Now, the thought is that seismic activity around the globe may play an important role in its variability.

The coupling of the lithosphere-atmosphere-ionosphere is a very complicated subject involving an array of physical effects and interactions on all levels from underground to the earth's magnetosphere. The volume of knowledge is so large that it is hard to research the topic in all directions. Starting in the 1930s, with observation of seismogenic electric fields, the idea of connecting lithospheric effects with the atmosphere has been a zone of scientific conflict. Because of the interdisciplinary aspects, the field is pedagogically off limits to many scientists. The theory requires knowledge of tectonics, seismology, atmospheric and ionospheric physics, chemistry, and electricity. Discussions between experts in these various groups often end up in disagreement.

For short-term prediction and accuracy, we are hardly farther along than were the ancient observers. However, the new theory of seismo-ionospheric coupling is very promising. Russian scientists, such as S.A. Pulinets, have called for a satellite system with ground-based measurements to analyze the anomalies and possibly turn them into a predictive method. Measuring only one parameter will not give enough confidence for prediction.

U.S. scientists are now examining this idea. An ionospheric perturbation was produced by the Coalinga, California earthquake of May 2, 1983, and detected by a network of high-frequency radio links in northern California. The more we look into the subject, the more we are likely to find evidence to support this phenomenon.

**Valuable anomalies**

The topic of earthquake prediction highlights the value of reported anomalies. We can learn valuable lessons about earth from observations made by average citizens and seasoned experts. A unifying theory to explain the reports of anomalies would give them credibility. While not all the anomalies can be adequately explained, it is the hope of those who report and study them that they will one day fit within a scientific framework.

When scientists Tributsch and Ikeya conducted their research into this subject, they were met with rejection from other professionals who did not judge citizen observation worthy of scientific research. Delving into these topics means grants are hard to come by and professional reputations can become tarnished. But with the support of the public and the mass media, science is expected to get to the root of these stories. Though scientists are reluctant to leave the safe environment of their practice, such an attitude undermines the strong public interest in the phenomenon. Curiously, cultural differences may play a role, with the western scientists less open to ideas that may be flavored with superstition.

The public expects science to develop ways to predict the occurrence of earthquakes. But science progresses in pulses. The previous failures in earthquake prediction do not necessarily mean that it can't be done; it means we may be looking in the wrong place for answers. There are many cases where adequate data for prediction existed prior to a quake, but it was not properly used to prepare the citizenry. As we saw in the Asian tsunami disaster, a coordinated effort is critical to success.

Earth processes are interconnected. It is heartening to see that we may be on a path now to understanding how the earth subtly alerts us to catastrophic events and thereby minimize or eliminate the associated suffering and death. That is the ultimate purpose of science.

## References

BBC News, (2006) "Plankton Blooms linked to quakes," May 9, 2006 from <news.bbc.co.uk/go/pr/fr/-/1/hi/sci/tech/4750557.stm> accessed on May 12, 2006.

Bolt, Bruce A., (1993) *Earthquakes*, W. H. Freeman and Company: New York.

Corliss, William R., (1983) *Earthquakes, Tides, Unidentified Sounds and Related Phenomena*, The Sourcebook Project: Glen Arm, MD.

Corliss, William R., (1995) *Handbook of Unusual Natural Phenomena: Eyewitness Accounts of Nature's Greatest Mysteries*, Gramercy Books/Random House.

Cyranoski, David, (2004) "A Seismic Shift in Thinking," *Nature* 431(7012): 1032-1034.

Geller, Robert J. et al., (1996) "Earthquakes Cannot Be Predicted," *Science* 275 (5306): 1616.

Gokhberg, M.B., V.A. Morgounov, and O.A. Pokhotelov, (1995) *Earthquake Prediction - Seismo-electromagnetic Phenomena*, Gordon & Breach Publishers.

Hough, Susan E., (2005) "Earthquakes: Predicting the Unpredictable?"

*Geotimes*, March 2005.

Ikeya, Motiji, (2004) *Earthquakes and Animals: From Folk Legends to Science*, World Scientific Publishing Co., Pte. Ltd.: Singapore.

Martinelli, Giovanni, (1998) "Earthquakes, Prediction" in *Sciences of the Earth: Volume 1*, Edited by G.A. Good. Garland Publishing: New York.

Oeser, E., (undated) "Historical Earthquake Theories" website <www. univie.ac.at/Wissenschaftstheorie/heat/heat-1/heat101f.htm>, accessed February 15, 2007.

O'Hanlon, Larry, (2003) "Earthquake Warnings in Ionosphere?" *Discovery News* (Discovery Channel), March 27, 2003.

Pennsylvania Department of Environmental Protection, (2002) "Pennsylvania Wells Record Effects of Alaskan Earthquake," *Update*, November 12, 2002.

Pulinets, S.A., (1998) "Strong Earthquake Prediction Possibility with the Help of Topside Sounding from Satellites," *Advances in Space Research*, Vol 21 No 3.

Pulinets, S.A., (1998) "Seismic activity as a source of the ionospheric variability" *Advances in Space Research*, Volume 22, No 6. <www. izmiran.rssi.ru/~pulse/COST%20SEISMO.pdf>.

Pulinets, Sergey, and Kirill Boyarchuk, (2004) *Ionospheric Precursors of Earthquakes*, Springer-Verlag: Berlin Heidelberg.

Science Blog <www.scienceblog.com/community/older/2002/A/20026958. html>.

Serebryakova, O. N., S. V. Bilichenko, V. M. Chmyrev, M. Parrot, J. L. Rauch, F. Lefeuvre, and O. A. Pokhotelov, (1992) "Electromagnetic elf radiation from earthquake regions as observed by low-altitude satellites," *Geophys. Res. Lett.*, 19(2), 91–94.

Tributsch, Helmut, (1982) *When the Snakes Awake: Animals and Earthquake Prediction*, MIT Press: Cambridge MA.

U.S. Geological Survey <earthquake.usgs.gov>.

Veysey, John, (2004) "Icelandic Water gives clues about quakes," *Milwaukee Journal Sentinel*, Aug 8, 2004 <www.jsonline.com/alive/news/ aug04/249223.asp> accessed Aug. 10, 2004.

*Washington Post*, <www.washingtonpost.com>, January 8, 2005, "Asia Quake Impacts Va. Well-Water Levels."

Wu, C., (1997) "Impurities give crystals that special glow," *Science News Online*, May 17, 1997, <www.sciencenews.org/pages/sn_arc97/5_17_ 97/fob2.htm>.

**SHARON HILL** is a geologist in Pennsylvania who takes a moderately skeptical approach to all things anomalous. She enjoys writing nontechnical articles for children and the general public to promote appreciation for science and natural phenomena.

# SARGON'S SEA SERPENT:
## THE FIRST SIGHTING IN CRYPTOZOOLOGY?
### BY ULRICH MAGIN

The Assyrian King Sargon had the first ever sighting of a sea serpent. Bernard Heuvelmans, in his *In the Wake of the Sea-Serpents*, writes: "Thus we learn that Sargon II, who reigned in Assyria from 722 to 705 B.C., saw a sea-serpent in the Mediterranean when sailing to Cyprus. This, so far as I know, is the first mention in history of a particular sighting of the subject of this book." (1) This information is of particular interest, as it is generally assumed that the history of the sea-serpent starts with Olaus Magnus' 1539 reference to such an animal on the Norwegian coast in his "Carta Marina." However, Heuvelmans gives no source for this report.

To learn more about Sargon's encounter, I checked the obvious ancient texts, such as Pliny, Herodotus etc., only to draw a blank. The only ancient text that refers to Sargon (20,1), as well as to a dragon (27,1; 30,6), a serpent (14,29; 27,1), the leviathan (27,1), and Cyprus (23,1; 23, 12) is the biblical Old Testament book of Isaiah, although the words do not occur in any context meaningful to our enquiry.

In an attempt to discover the origin of the story – either Heuvelmans' source or the ancient text itself – I wrote letters asking for information to *Fortean Times* (2), to the paleocryptozoologist Adrienne Mayor, and to Karl Shuker, and I published several earlier versions of this article with my preliminary findings in various editions of the German cryptozoology magazine *Pterodactylus*. (3) I also posted on several discussion boards for archaeology and Assyrology on the internet but did not receive a single answer.

*Tiamat's Brood* by Alastair McBeath, the only book ever published about dragons in old Mesopotamia, does not mention the incident. (4) It seemed that no one knew – or cared – where this piece of sea-serpent lore had originated. Yet it had already filtered into the literature on the subject and was being taken as fact, for example, by Paul Lester in his sociological interpretation of sea-serpent history. (5)

**A Tale of Two Sargons**

The problem was further complicated by the only mention of the creature that appeared to be indepentent of Heuvelmans, a paper by paleocryptozoologist Adrienne Mayor in *Cryptozoology*. In this article, Mayor lists all ancient mentions of sea-monsters, among them – yet without any reference – a "Sargon of Akkad inscription." (6)

Now, Sargon of Akkad (or Sargon the Great) is not the same person as Sargon II of Assyria. Sargon of Akkad lived around 2300 BC while Sargon II ruled in the 8th century BC. These are two different rulers – but which one saw the sea-serpent?

Sargon is the biblical version of the Akkadian name Sarru-kin (rightful ruler or king). It was this Sargon of Akkad (ca. 2330-2280 BC) who founded the first Semitic dynasty in Babylonia. There are no historical documents from his time, all we know about him comes from later mythological tales.

These legends make him the son of a priestess who left him drifting (his father had deserted her) in a basket on the Euphrates River. There he was found by Akki, the irrigator, who adopted and educated him. (7) This story, historians believe, influenced the similar but later tale about Moses.

Sargon became the cupbearer of the Sumerian king Ur-Zababa of Kus, then ruler of that city state when – aided by Semitic allies – he overthrew Ur-Zababa and took the throne. He then attacked king Lugalsagesi of Uruk, was victorious, and finally conquered the whole south of Babylonia. In his third year of reign, he marched through Tuttul on the Euphrates until he came to the Mediterranean, the Cedar Forest (Lebanon), and Asia Minor, where, as the Battle Epic tells, he fought with mythical monsters on land, not in the sea.

With his many campaigns, Sargon created the first Mesopotamian Empire. He ruled from his (as yet undiscovered) capital Akkade, and his reign was threatened until his death by uprisings. (8)

All of this biography, however, is pieced together from later sources: "Sargon is known almost entirely from the legends and tales that followed his reputation through 2,000 years of cuneiform Mesopotamian history, and not from documents that were written during his lifetime," as the *Encyclopaedia Britannica* stresses. (9)

So even if Adrienne Mayor were right, a sea-serpent sighting by Sargon would hardly be available from one of his inscriptions, as there aren't any! And more: even if it is sometimes stated that Sargon crossed the Western Sea [the Mediterranean] and landed at Cyprus and Crete (10), there is no evidence for this, and the claim is rejected by archaeologists.

As so little is known about Sargon the Great, it is no wonder that the only "biography" I could find was a very colorful historical novel which certainly doesn't guarantee well researched archaeological facts. Tantalizingly, this novel, *Lugal* by Josef Nyary, mentions a monster that appeared during Sargon's reign. The novelist claims that Sargon for the first time felt that he was born to be king "... in spring, on the first of the seven days of the month Nisan, in the year that the giant red serpent disported itself in the Tigris." (11) Whether or not there is actually an inscription that refers to the event, or whether Nyary invented it, I could not find. As this episode is about a river monster, not a sea-monster, it cannot be based on the inscription listed by Mayor, which is doubtful in itself.

As it is generally agreed that Sargon the Great left no inscriptions, and Heuvelmans expressly refers to Sargon II, it is obvious that Mayor made a mistake and mixed up and confused the two kings. We need to closer look at the life of Sargon II to see whether we can find any text that reveals more about his supposed sighting.

### Sargon's Life and His Voyage to Cyprus

Sargon II of Assyria (721-705 BC) possibly had no rights to, and usurped, the Assyrian throne. "Upon his accession to the throne or his usurpation, Sargon experienced a major domestic crises ... The circumstances of Sargon's accession to the throne are most obscure." (12) Sargon claimed to be of noble descent, but it is more likely that he had only been a higher official under King Shalmaneser IV. In any case, by adopting the name Sarru-kin (rightful king), and by therefore referring back to Sargon the Great, he certainly hinted that he had all the rights to the throne.

Like his namesake, Sargon II was a great warlord. It would be too cumbersome to list all his expeditions and campaigns, as he enlarged the Assyrian Empire each year (13) – in 720 he conquered Syria and Egypt (and on this occasion deported the people of Samaria, as told in the Bible), in 717 he turned Karkemis into an Assyrian province, then he was victorious over king Mita (the Midas of myths) and subdued the whole of southeast Anatolia. His eighth expedition led to the conquest of the Urartu Empire (around Mt. Ararat where the Bible says the Ark stranded), and Sargon, whose war reports and annals are regarded as stylistic masterpieces, described his exploits in 712 in a long "letter to the Gods." His empire finally secure at the eastern and western frontiers, Sargon II attacked Babylonia and conquered it. King Marduk-apla-iddina (14) fled and Sargon took his throne.

Sargon was finally killed in his last campaign against Tabal (15): "The death of a king on a battlefield, killed in action, is as yet unheard in the history of Mesopotamia. Sennacherib had to investigate the hidden reasons of his father's death in order to find out what were the sins (hitati) of Sargon." (16) "His son Sennacherib believed Sargon's death was a punishment from the gods and left his corpse unburied. [He also] left Sargon's new city unfinished and built a huge palace at Niniveh." (17) (Sargon had started the construction of a new capital, Dur-Sarrukin, "Sargon City," at modern Khorsabad, some 15 miles north of Mossul. The site was excavated by the French archaeologist Paul Botto in 1843-1844; he later published his findings in 5 volumes.) An encounter with a dragon might have been regarded as a bad omen to be fixed in writing by Sennacherib, yet I could find no such text.

Sargon II subdued Cyprus, Assyrian Iatnan(a) or Yatnan(a), in the year 708/707 BC. This "Cypriotic episode is related in numerous inscriptions, all written immediately after the island's conquest," writes Nadav Na'Aman of Tel Aviv University. "One group mentions that the island of Cyprus marks the westernmost limit of the Assyrian empire, and a second group calls Sargon 'subduer of the seven kings of Ia,' a district of the land of Iadnanna. Some inscriptions reveal how fright fell upon the Cypriotic kings and they brought their gifts to Sargon and 'kissed my feet.' Concrete details of the conquest of the island are related only in the Khorsabad annals, which are badly broken." (18)

The main sources for Sargon's visit or expedition to Cyprus are the Annals of Khorsabad, a stela erected at Kittim, modern Larnaca, as well as several inscriptions in the palace at Dur-Sarrukin.

The "great inscription in the palace of Khorsabad" is Sargon's most detailed account of his conquest of Cyprus, and it reads (as translated by Dr. Julius Oppert): "43 And the seven Kings of the country of Iahnagi, of the country of Iatnan (who have established and extended their dwellings at a distance of seven days' navigation in the midst of the sea of the setting sun, and whose name from the most ancient ages until the renewal of the lunar period, none of the Kings my fathers in Assyria and Chaldea had heard), had been told of my lofty achievements in Chaldea and Syria, and my glory, which had spread afar to the midst of the sea. They subdued their pride and humbled themselves; they presented themselves before me at Babylon, bearing metals, gold, silver, vases, ebony wood, and the manufactures of their country; they kissed my feet." (19)

From this, it is evident that Sargon had never been in Cyprus but that the coalition of Cypriotic kings had visited him in his empire to subdue themselves!

The stela erected by Sargon in Kitium/Citium after his "conquest" also doesn't mention a sea-serpent. "The triumphant stela on which he related that his vessels have vanquished Cyprus" (20) is only "recording the fact that seven Cypriot kings had paid him homage; subsequent Assyrian documents speak of 11 tributary kingdoms: the seven (Curium, Paphos, Marion, Soli, Lapithos, Salamis, Amathus) plus Kitium, Kyrenia, Tamassos, and Idalium." (21)

I consulted all four volumes I was able to trace that contain translations of Sargon's texts (Tadmor, Lyon, Winckler, and Lie), to see whether I could find a hint or any information on anything that might have resulted in the information that Sargon spotted a sea-serpent on his voyage to Cyprus. Those texts, originally published in German, are here in my English translation.

Dr. D. G. Lyon (22) assembles several Khorsabad texts, the

so-called cylinder inscription (of which there are four copies), the bull inscription, a bronce tablet, a silver tablet, a gold tablet, and the so-called Antimon inscription. Cyprus (and possibly Greece) is mentioned in only two of these texts.

We read in the so-called cylinder inscription, line 21 (23): "le'i tamhari sa ina kabal tamtim Jamna'a sandanis kima nune ibaruma upsasihu Kue u Surri = (Sargon), strong in battle, who in the midst of the Sea the Jonian ... fished like fishes, and who pacified the land of Kue and the city of Tyrus, ..."

And in the bull inscription on a plate fixed to a monumental bull in Sargon's palace, line 25 (24): "ekmute sa Jamna'a sa kabal tamtim kima nune ibaru ...VII sarrani sa Ja'i nage sa Ad(?)nana sa malak VII ume ina kabal tamti ... = ... who fished the Jonian in the midst of the Sea like fishes, ... who subdued the 7 kings of Ja', a district of Cyprus, whose dwellings are at a distance of 7 days navigation in the western sea ..."

Hugo Winckler's book (25) is another edition of all the inscriptions from Khorsabad: it includes not only the Annals, but also all mural inscriptions, texts from ground plates, propaganda inscriptions, as well as single lines on bricks. The subjugation of the kings of Cyprus is often mentioned, but there is no single allusion to a sea-serpent or water monster. (26)

Arthur Gottfred Lie (27) only gives variants of the Annal texts already quoted:

"457. ... seven kings

458. of Ia'u, province of Adnana, who seven days distance in the midst of the sea where the sun is setting had settled

459. and whose dwelling is distant, who from far-off days to the kings ...."

All of Sargon's reports on his conquest of Cyprus, therefore, are boringly repetitive and similar. None mentions a sea-serpent, and there is only a slim chance that a line I missed on an inscription I wasn't aware of would add any substantial text on this endeavor. Furthermore, as the kings of Cyprus traveled to Babylonia, Sargon II most likely never went to the Mediterranean island himself. Joseph Greene of Harvard Semitic Museum stresses that "nothing in the island's archeological record can be construed as evidence for a late eighth century BC Assyrian armed invasion, military occupation or civil administration of Cyprus. ... Sargon did not actually claim to have invaded and occupied the island after the manner of his conquests on the mainland. He stated only he subdued its seven kings and forced them to pay tribute." (28)

If Sargon II never went to Cyprus, it is most unlikely that he met with a sea-serpent on this imaginary voyage. We can conclude that there is no text by Sargon II that describes such an observation as Heuvelmans alludes to.

So, there is no evidence that Sargon II ever journeyed to Cyprus and less so that he encountered a monstrous serpent while at sea. As this is the case, then how did this myth start?

**How the Story Developed**

You can now forget all these historical aspects as they have nothing to do with Sargon's sea-serpent. I only came across the true history of his "sighting" while I researched a completely different matter and chanced upon a reference to the work of one John Ashton in A. C. Oudemans classic and monumental study of the sea-serpent.

As it appears, the claim that Sargon met with a sea serpent was first offered by John Ashton. In his book *Curious Creatures in Zoology*, (29) first published in 1889, he deals with a vide variety of legends about real and imaginary beings, among them the sea-serpent. At the very start of this chapter, Ashton reproduces a drawing of an eel-like animal from a relief at Khorsabad depicting Sargon's journey to Cyprus: "On the antiquity of the belief in the Sea-Serpent there can be no doubt, for it is represented on the walls of the Assyrian palace of Khorsabad, more than once, in the sculpture representing the voyage of Sargon to Cyprus."

It should be noted, however, that Ashton quickly contradicts what he wrote a few lines later: "These ... were doubtless marine snakes, which are still in existence, and are found in the Indian Ocean."

Ashton includes a pencil sketch of the creature: it shows a serpentine animal with large, diamond-shaped scales and a raised, elongated head. The forked tongue that is commonly used to indicate a serpent is absent, however.

A. C. Oudemans, author of the most authoritative study of the sea-serpent problem, had to agree with Ashton for dismissing, but not for bringing up, Sargon's Khorsabad relief in the discussion. In 1892 he says about Ashton's claim in his classic *The Great Sea-Serpent* (30): "The illustrations which accompany this part [Ashton's chapter on the sea-serpent] are: 1. A representation of a piece of sculpture on a wall of the Assyrian palace at Khorsabad, which I believe, has nothing to do with the sea-serpent, but which is a bad drawing of a *Hydrophis.*"

*Hydrophis*, the true sea-snake, only lives in the Indian Ocean, and Sargon II is depicted sailing the Mediterranean. So the identity suggested by both Ashton and Oudemans cannot apply. But Assyrian reliefs often show a wide variety of marine animals, among them snake-like fish, and the sculptures may intend only to show a vague general image of an elongated fish or eel, without the intending to illustrate a definite species. As Ashton says it is shown "more than once," it is not depicted as a horrible monster or portentous omen anyway, just as a normal fish. Indeed, several of the Assyrian reliefs on display at the British Museum in London have these snake-like fish swimming in the water when depicting rivers, lakes, or the sea. They are a symbol rather than a journalistic representation.

From Ashton, Sargon's "monster" obviously made its way into several general articles on sea-serpents. One of these is "Das Rätsel der Seeschlange," by Ch. Fr. Holder and David Starr Jordan, published in a 1913 edition of the German popular science magazine *Kosmos*. (31) It is a translation from a chapter of their book *Fish Stories*. (32)

Ch. Fr. Holder and David Starr Jordan start their chapter – I retranslate from the German – with a paragraph which appears to have Ashton as source, yet they transform his interpretation of a depiction into an actual report: "The sea serpent has a long pedigree. ... On the walls of the Assyrian palace at Khorsabad one sees a sea serpent which a certain Sargon spotted 2600 years ago on a trip to Cyprus."

Neither this source nor Ashton's book appear in Heuvelman's bibliography; he may therefore have copied his information on Sargon from still another, similar source. But I am very certain that Ashton was the first to interpret the eel-like images as a sea-serpent, and that Holder and Jordan turned this into the claim that Sargon had actually observed such a monster.

Sargon did not see a sea-serpent and Heuvelmans did not make the sighting up; he simply copied a secondary source without checking it, as he usually did, and then presented it as fact and as if he had worked with a primary source. This is, it seems, the path the story followed and found its way into Heuvelman's book. From images of serpentine fishes, thought by a single author to possibly refer to a sea-serpent, to the world's first sighting report of a sea-serpent, it took only three steps – Chinese whispers in cryptozoology!

It is therefore impossible to find Sargon's report, because there never was any. The story developed from a naive and innocent claim made in 1889 (which was retracted a few lines later and disputed anyway, and which we know is false). A German saying describes exaggeration as "turning a mouse into an elephant," and here we have an eel turned into the mightiest creature of the ocean!

This study shows that, unless an author quotes his source, we should be prepared for mistakes to creep into the story as it is copied down the line. Also, when quoting a primary source from a secondary one, it is important to always quote the secondary source as well. Third, when a sighting is summarized, one should always go to the original report, as the summary will make mistakes and assumptions that are not included in the original versions.

1889: "On the antiquity of the belief in the Sea-Serpent there can be no doubt, for it is *represented* on the walls of the Assyrian palace of Khorsabad, *more than once*, in the sculpture representing the voyage of Sargon to Cyprus."

1913: "On the walls of the Assyrian palace at Khorsabad one sees *a sea serpent* which a certain Sargon *spotted* 2600 years ago on a trip to Cyprus."

1968: "Thus we learn that *Sargon* II, who reigned in Assyria from 722 to 705 B.C., *saw a sea-serpent* in the Mediterranean when sailing to Cyprus. This, so far as I know, is the first mention in history of *a particular sighting* of the subject of this book."

**Postscript**

In the course of my research, I came across two very early

references to large marine creatures which both antedate the Sargon claim, but which are equally problematic. I give them here for completeness sake, but I am convinced that both have nothing to do with the modern sea-serpent problem.

**The Story of the Shipwrecked Sailor**

There is an ancient Egyptian tale that just might be related to a belief in serpentine large marine creatures. In the Middle Kingdom, Egyptian literature was at its apex. (33) One text, the "shipwrecked sailor," is contained in a papyrus kept in the Moscow Museum and was written during the reign of Pharaoh Sesostris III (19th century BC). (34) An official of the king tells a nobleman, whose journey to Nubia failed, about his own shipwreck.

The storyteller is on a large boat in the Red Sea on his voyage to the Pharaoh's mines when a storm destroys the ship. He alone, clinging to a log, is able to save his life on a deserted island. This island is a paradise, and the shipwrecked sailor makes an offering to the Gods when: "Suddenly I heard a noise as of thunder, which I thought to be that of a wave of the sea. The trees shook, and the earth was moved. I uncovered my face, and I saw that a serpent drew near. He was thirty cubits long, and his beard greater than two cubits; his body was as overlaid with gold, and his color as that of true lazuli. He coiled himself before me."

One of Heuvelman's merhorses coming ashore? This is unlikely, as the serpent began to speak to the shipwrecked sailor. "He then opened his mouth, while I lay on my face before him, and he said to me, 'What has brought you, what has brought you, little one, what has brought you? If you say not speedily what has brought you to this isle, I will make you know yourself; as a flame you shall vanish, if you tell me not something I have not heard, or which I knew not, before you.'"

In great detail the shipwrecked sailor now tells of his journey through the storm, and how he was able to save his life. The serpent pities him and explains that he has become stranded on the isle of Ka. The Ka is one of the several souls that the ancient Egyptians thought live in our bodies and survive death, so our sailor really is in paradise, an isle of the afterlife. The serpent tells him that originally there had been 75 snakes on the island, but the fire of a falling star has killed all of them but him. The serpent predicts that the sailor will return to the Pharaoh, and so it happens. (35)

Thirty cubits equals 16 meters (53 ft), and the two cubits of the beard are about one yard in length. This beard was a privilege of Gods and kings and this, combined with the sailor falling on his knees before it, identifies the fire-spouting serpent as an otherwordly or godly being.

Even if the description of a large serpent with a mane which can move on dry land seems to indicate one of the sea-serpent species identified by Heuvelmans, this is clearly no Egyptian eyewitness report of an unusual encounter in the Red Sea but a mythological tale about a dead man's journey into the afterlife and back.

## The Sea-monster of Tiglath-pileser

The Assyrian king Tiglath-Pileser (1115-1077 BC) possibly did meet with a sea-monster. In a description made many years after his death on a broken obelisk by King Asshurnazirpal III, the later credits his forefather with the slaying of a sea-monster. Tiglath-Pileser, after having made an expedition to the Levante coast, sailed in ships of Arvad (a Phoenician city) and slew a *nakhiru* (literally, a "nostril animal," "merhorse," or "blower") in the Western Sea, the Mediterranean. (36)

The name certainly is suggestive, but the only certainty we have is that it refers to "a sea-monster of some kind." Around 1900, Sayce suggested it meant dolphin, and Paul Hamupt, in a treatise on Jonah's whale, in 1907 positively identified the hakhiru with a sperm-whale. This idea is still valid today, as much progress has been made in Assyrian studies. In 1996, the Italian scholar Claudio Saporetti published an analysis of several sources to confirm that *nakhiru* was "a cetacean," although it was difficult to pin down any species. (37)

## Notes

1. Heuvelmans, Bernard: *In the Wake of the Sea-Serpents.* Hill & Wang, New York 1968, p. 82.
2. *Fortean Times* 139, p. 53
3. *Pterodactylus* 10, 2002, p. 35-37; *Pterodactylus* 11, 2002; *Pterodactylus*

23, 2005, p. 20

4. Alastair McBeath: *Tiamat's Brood: An Investigation into the Dragons of Ancient Mesopotamia*. Dragon's Head Press, London 1999.

5. Paul Lester: *The Great Sea Serpent Controversy: A Cultural Study*. Protean Pubs, Birmingham 1984, p. 3.

6. Adrienne Mayor: "Paleocryptozoology: A Call for Collaboration between Classicists and Cryptozoologists." *Cryptozoology* 8, 1989, p. 23.

7. Cf. <www.fordham.edu/halsall/ancient/2300sargon1.html>.

8. Der Kleine Pauly. Alfred Druckenmüller, Munich 1975, vol. 4, col. 1554/1555.

9. Sargon in: britannica.com.

10. Beck, Sanderson: "Ethics of Sumer, Babylon, and Hittites." <www.san. beck.org/EC3-Sumer.html#2>.

11. Josef Nyary: Lugal. Bastei Lübbe: Bergisch Gladbach n.d. (1991?), p. 18.

12. H. Tadmor: "The Campaigns of Sargon II of Assyria." *Journal of Cuneiform Studies* 12, 22-40; 77-100 (1958), p. 37 and note 138.

13. A list of the campaigns can be found in Tadmor.

14. The Merodach-Baladan of the Bible, cf. 2 Kings 20,12 and Isaiah 39,1.

15. Der Kleine Pauly. Munich, Alfred Druckenmüller, 1975, vol. 4, col. 1555.

16. Tadmor, p. 97.

17. Back, Sanderson: "Ethics of Assyrian, Babylonian, and Persian Empires," <www.san.beck.org/EC6-Assyria.html>.

18. Na'Aman, Nadav: "The Conquest of Iadnana According to Sargon II's Inscriptions." *XLVe Recontre Assyriologique Internationale*, Cambridge, MA, July 5-8 1998, <www-oi.uchicago.edu/OI/DEPT/RA/rai/45_Abstracts. html>.

19. Oppert, Julius (ed): "Great Inscriptions in the Palace of Khorsabad", in: *Records of the Past*, vol. 9. Samuel Bagster and Sons, London 1877.

20. See <www.noteaccess.com/Texts/OAntiquities/Pa.htm>.

21. See <www.cypnet.com/.ncyprus/asur.html>.

22. Dr. D. G. Lyon: *Keilschrifttexte Sargon's Königs von Assyrien*. J. C. Hinrich'sche Buchhandlung, Leipzig 1883.

23. Lyon, p. 32/33.

24. Lyon, p. 42/43.

25. Winckler, Hugo: *Die Keilschrifttexte Sargons*. Band I. Eduard Pfeiffer, Leipzig 1889.

26. Winckler's translation only repeats lines already quoted, the description was rather standardized, cf. his p. 65, 83, 85, 99, 127, 137, 139, 143, 149,

151, 159, 183, 181.

27. Arthur Gottfred Lie: *The Inscriptions of Sargon II King of Assyria. Part I: The Annals.* Paris: Librairie Orientaliste Paul Geuthner 1929, S. 69.

28. Greene, Joseph: "The Subjugation of Iadnana by Sargon II: The Archaeological Evidence." *XLVe Recontre Assyriologique Internationale*, Cambridge, MA, July 5-8 1998, <www-oi.uchicago.edu/OI/DEPT/RA/rai/45_Abstracts.html>.

29. John Ashton: *Curious Creatures in Zoology.* Cassell, New York 1890; electronic reprint by Arment Biological Press, Landisville, PA 2000, p. 268-278. Ashton also mentions a merman on the same sculpture, obviously he had a recent press account or book on the excavations as his source: "But, undoubtedly," he writes, "the earliest representation of the real Merman – half-man, half-fish – comes to us from the uncovered palace of Khorsabad. On a portion of its sculptured walls is a representation of Sargon, the father of Sennacherib, sailing on his expedition to Cyprus, B.C. 720 – on which occasion he had wooden images of the gods made and thrown overboard in order to accompany him on his voyage. Among these is Hea, or Oannes, which I venture to assert is the first representation of a Merman."– Ashton, p. 127.

30. A. C. Oudemans: *The Great Sea-Serpent.* Brill, Luzak & Co., Leyden 1892, p. 378.

31. Ch. Fr. Holder and David Starr: "Das Rätsel der Seeschlange." *Kosmos* 1913, p. 287-290. The German text is: "Die Seeschlange kann sich eines uralten Stammbaums rühmen. Schon vor vielen Jahrhunderten bildete sie die Grundlage für Berichte von Meerungeheuern. An den Wänden des assyrischen Palastes zu Chorsabad sieht man eine Seeschlange dargestellt, die ein gewisser Sargon vor nunmehr 2600 Jahren auf seiner Fahrt nach Zypern gesehen hatte."

32. Ch. Fr. Holder and David Starr Jordan: *Fish Stories.* H. Holt & Company, New York n.d. I have not had the opportunity to consult the American original.

33. Tyldesley, Joyce: Hatschepsut. Heyne, Munich 2001, p. 35-36

34. Posting by Martin Pohl in the Forum für alternative und klassische Archäologie, 12 July 2001.

35. Quoted from Uther, Hans-Jörg (ed): Altägyptische Märchen – Mythen und andere volkstümliche Erzählungen. Introduction, translation and commentary by Emma Brunner-Traut. Augsburg: Bechtermünz 1998 (Original: 1963); the story is also included in: Mythen alter Kulturen. Stuttgart: Reclam 1996; Petrie, Flinders: Egyptian Tales; Tappan, Eva March: The World's Story. vol. III. Egypt, Africa, and Arabia, p. 41-46;

English version at <www.fordham.edu/halsall/ancient/2200shipwreck.html>.

36. Edward S. Ellis & Charles F. Horne, "The Story of the Greatest Nations and the World's Famous Events, "vol. 1, 1913, quoted in: <www.publicbookshelf.com/public_html/The_Story_of_the_Greatest_Nations_and_the_Worlds_Famous_Events_Vol_1/tiglathp_ic.html>; <aina.org/aol/peter/brief.htm>; Charles Kimball: "New peoples, new nations, part II "on <hynahost.net/education/berosus2/neareast/ne02b.html; pw1.netcom.com/~ye-stars/tmacons.htm>.

37. Claudio Saporetti: Il problema del *nakhiru*. in: Enrico Acquario (ed): Studi in onore di Sabato Moscati, Instituti Editoriali e Poligrafici Internazionali, Pisa 1996.

Note: Several of the internet sources were accessed to a few years ago and they may no longer be valid.

**ULRICH MAGIN**, born in 1962, is author of several books on cryptozoology, close encounter UFO cases, ley lines, and a biography of Charles Fort, as well as of many articles in major fortean magazines: *Fortean Times, INFO Journal, Pursuit, The Ley Hunter, Fortean Studies,* and *Strange Magazine.* He is primarily interested in lake monsters and he lives with his partner near Stuttgart, Germany.

# MEDIEVAL MYSTICISM AND ITS EMPIRICAL KINSHIP TO AYAHUASCA
## By Victoria Alexander

Ayahuasca is used as a religious sacrament primarily in South America. While non-native users know of the spiritual applications of ayahuasca, a less well-known traditional usage focuses on the medicinal properties of ayahuasca. Its purgative properties are highly important (la Purga, "the purge"). Sections of ayahuasca vine are boiled with leaves from any of a large number of potential admixture plants (such as Psychotria viridis, chakruna or chaliponga) resulting in a tea that contains the powerful hallucinogenic alkaloids harmine, harmaline, d-tetrahydroharmine, and dimethyltryptamine (DMT). Dimethyltryptamine closely resembles serotonin and has been discovered to be a component of normal mammalian metabolism, an endogenous hallucinogen. This brew has been used in the Amazon for millennia in order to heal, divine, and worship.

Most ayahuasqueros (ayahuasca shamans) and others working with the brew claim the *B. caapi* vine to be the defining ingredient; according to them, it is not ayahuasca unless *B. caapi* is in the brew. The vine is considered to be the "spirit" of ayahuasca, the gatekeeper and guide to the otherworldly realms.

My advocacy for ayahuasca – not as a visionary tool solely the domain of shamans and medicine men but as an agent for mystical experience available to everyone – has directed my pursuit of the medicine. In my lifelong study of the mystical experiences of Catholic saints, primarily focusing on those who lived during the Middle Ages, it was evident that thousands of dedicated men and women chose drastic methods to achieve a union with God. Today, we are able to have visions and see God through the less drastic, but just as controversial, use of ayahuasca.

Patrons of the sacred medicine consistently compare the visions experienced by mystics with those produced by ingesting ayahuasca, either under the guidance of shamans or through the Santo Daime Doctrine. Alex Polari de Alverga, a leader of the Santo Daime Doctrine, said: "In fact, the mirações we experience in ritual works are remarkably similar to visions and ecstatic states described by saints of many religions." ("The Santo Daime Doctrine. An Interview with Alex Polari de Alverga," by Gary Dale Richman, *Shaman's Drum*, Number 22, Winter 1990-91.)

In an essay titled "Do Drugs Have Religious Import?" Huston Smith, a great champion of the religious significance of entheogenic plants and chemicals, wrote: "But given the right set and setting, the drugs can induce religious experiences that are indistinguishable from such experiences that occur spontaneously." (*Cleansing the Doors of Perception: The Religious Significance of Entheogenic Plants and Chemicals,* by Huston Smith, Jeremy P. Tarcher/Putnam, 2000.)

I will briefly outline here the practices of mystics and saints and present an archetypal pattern that can also be found in ayahuasca usage. However, I would like to echo the words of my friend Kenneth Ring who in stressing certain linkages between near-death experiences and UFO experiences, wrote: "I make no claim that *all* varieties of these two phenomena are thus entwined." Instead I would like to submit here a discussion along the lines of Ring's "framework for a partial conceptual integration of two nonordinary experiences previously held to be quite separate and unrelated." In doing so, I hope to build a theoretical bridge unifying mysticism and ayahuasca. Like Ring, I found there are "obvious differences" in the two types of experiences I am comparing and yet, similarly, a "deep structure" that indicates "important commonalities." ("Near-Death and UFO Encounters as Shamanic Initiations: Some Conceptual and Evolutionary Implications," by Kenneth Ring, *ReVISION*, Vol. 11, No. 3. Winter 1989.)

What is evidently clear about these two nonordinary states is that neither can be manipulated or harnessed. There are signposts and guidelines, but the journey is singularly individual.

Ayahuasca is an instrument that can be used by anyone to seek a direct experience with the spirit world, God, or for profound personal transformation. The democracy of ayahuasca is what gives it power. What gives ayahuasca kinship to mysticism is that it can be used as a tool for religious exploration. Spiritual seekers during the Middle Ages used the only avenue available to them to achieve their religious purposes. The fact that mystical experience was impossible to control led to its diminished significance within the Catholic Church. And while ayahuasca is illegal in the U.S., Americans can still find ways to experience it.

Modern scholars have condemned medieval religious practices and have brutally criticized them. But in the pursuit of spiritual ecstasy and revelation, I do not.

The fact that prayers and pleas to Jesus Christ and the Virgin Mary dominated the ayahuasca ceremonies I attended at a SpiritQuest retreat in Iquitos, Peru makes the relationship of ayahuasca to Catholic mysticism all the more striking. In their paper "Identifying Spiritual Content in Reports from Ayahuasca Sessions," (*International Journal of Transpersonal Studies*, 2000, Volume 19, pp. 59-76), Stanley Krippner and Joseph Sulla write: "There has been little rigorous research on the spiritual content of *ayahuasca* sessions, despite the tribal use of this herbal concoction and the existence of three Brazilian churches in which *ayahuasca* is considered a sacrament." I was not aware of the strong influence that Catholicism had on Peruvian curanderos and how harmoniously it shaped their ayahuasca ceremonies. With more and more Westerners traveling to South America for the intent purpose of experiencing ayahuasca visions, it is now possible to achieve what religious scholars have termed "Grand Mysticism."

**The Medieval Pathway**

In the Middle Ages, if one wanted to know God firsthand and have mystical experiences, one embarked on a life of rigid asceticism. Extreme fasting, intense mortification of the body, arduous prayer, self-denial, and sacrifice were all deemed the consecrated pathway. Christian ascetic practices began in the third century in the deserts of Egypt and flourished until the fourteenth century. Asceticism worked: Tens of thousands of men and women willingly lived the cruel reality of desert monasticism. The practitioner entered a visionary world far more satisfying than the material world. (I highly recommend *The God-Possessed* by Jacques Lacarrìere, George Allen & Unwin Ltd, 1963, for an informative study of Christian desert ascetic practices.)

Today, contemporary Western religions have denounced self-mortification as a tool for experiencing God, the exception being the religious community known as Opus Dei, which advocates fasting and corporal mortifications even for its secular members. Outside the realm of religious fasts such as the Catholic Church's observation of Lent, abstaining from any food for long periods of time is considered a psychological aberration and denounced as a medical eating disorder. The religious significance of ascetic fasting has been vilified and the Catholic Church no longer officially sanctions self-mortification. Nevertheless, Christianity rests firmly on a foundation of asceticism.

Opus Die was founded in Madrid, Spain, on October 2, 1928, by Blessed Josemaria Escriva. Nearly 80,000 people from around the world belong to this Prelature of the Catholic Church. Regarding ascetic practices, Blessed Josemaria Escriva wrote: "No ideal becomes a reality without sacrifice. Deny yourself. It is so beautiful to be a victim!" Opus Dei members practice corporal mortifications by using the cilice and the discipline. The cilice is a spiked chain worn around the upper thigh for two hours a day. The cilice provides a painful form of suffering and leaves tiny prick holes in the flesh. The discipline is a cord-like whip used on the buttocks and back once a week. A member of Opus Dei may ask permission to use the cilice and whip more often. Blessed Josemaria Escriva was particularly devoted to the constant use of the discipline and the walls of his bathroom were said to be covered in his blood. Notwithstanding the Opus Dei practices, the modern Catholic Church has set aside ascetic exercises as counter-productive to achieving spiritual progress.

For more than nine hundred years such religious practices as extreme bodily mortifications and self-starvation were celebrated as a means to chastise the body and bring it closer to God. These harsh disciplines successfully brought about a union with God, as evidenced in the lives of mystics and saints whose testament proclaimed their efficiency. For individuals who chose the path of the religious life, it was vital to suffer physical pain in order to experience God. By reducing the body's sensation of pleasure to nothing, one was able to attain ecstasy, rapture, and profound visions of God.

One method, flagellation, holds a secure place in religious history as a hallowed path. In the Middle Ages, the abbess of a convent was customarily expected to whip the novices and was regularly required to submit herself, in private or in public, to a scourging. Some convents trained members especially for the gruesome undertaking of scourging, guaranteeing for a more oppressive flagellation. In medieval monasteries, monks wore a special shirt that opened in the back, so a flogging was more readily accessible. Each monastic order, for both sexes, had a flogging schedule that varied from once, twice or three times a week. The Capuchin Friars were required to discipline themselves every day. Young monks crowned themselves with thorns or walked with their arms crossed and tied to a piece of wood. There is an enormous amount of literature on the lives of religious men who whipped themselves in frenzied, bloodthirsty penances. Even the great founder of the Jesuit order, St. Ignatius Loyola, was said to have wholeheartedly used the whip. According to George Ryley Scott, author of *The History of Corporal Punishment* (Senate, 1968), Loyola's Jesuit priests (it is now diversely claimed) became "addicted to whipping."

This Catholic Church's tradition can be traced to no less a luminary than St. Paul, who was himself an advocate and self-flagellator: "I chastise my body and bring it into subjection..." (I Cor. 9:27). The grotesque devices fashioned by the religious for self-torture also showed a high degree of imagination and purposeful intent on causing the most spectacular suffering. But mystical experiences, achieved by any means, are not considered "proof of sanctity" when evaluating candidates for sainthood. In *Making Saints: How The Catholic Church Determines Who Becomes A Saint, Who Doesn't, and Why*, author Kenneth L. Woodward is quite clear in his assessment of the Church's position. Woodward writes that the "saint-makers seem downright suspicious of causes involving mystical phenomena, and anxious to dispel any notion that mystics are inherently different from other saints." Further, Woodward states that the Church regards all mystical gifts and wonder-working as "graces given for the benefit of the Christian community" as a whole and not for the fulfillment of the individual mystic.

These extreme practices were tolerated because its effectiveness was not only evident in the works and life of the mystic but served their communities in very practical ways. The benefits derived from the prayers, miraculous healings, and social services of these religious persons were so great that when a "living saint" died, communities nearly went to war over their remains. The demand for relics is the subject of a fascinating book, *Furta Sacra: Thefts of Relics in the Central Middle Ages* by Patrick J. Geary (Princeton University Press, 1978.) Geary writes: "Upon his [Saint Abbanus, a sixth-century Irish saint] death in the monastery of Magh-Arnuidhe which he had founded, citizens of Ceall-Abbain, his birthplace, came and stole his body. The result was almost a war, but the two opposing forces met and presented their arguments before coming to blows."

To re-emphasize this important point, I'd like to mention two other incidents that clearly indicate the significance over saintly remains. These appear in Ronald C. Finucane's *Miracles and Pilgrims: Popular Beliefs in Medieval England* (St Martin's Press, 1977). (1) "For financial as well as other reasons some famous relics caused prolonged disputes between towns or rival monasteries. Glastonbury and Canterbury contended for St. Dunstan's [d. 988] corpse into the sixteenth century and Dorchester and Winchester both claimed the bones of Bishop Birinus [d. 650], just as in the early Middle Ages the monks of Poitiers and Tours disputed energetically about the body of St. Martin [d. 397]." (2) "The body [Louis of Toulouse, d. 1297] remained enshrined at Marseilles until 1423 when the Aragonese, who had stormed the walls, were said to have agreed to spare the city in exchange for Louis's remains."

The spiritual fruits of harsh self-mortification have been known and widely used since antiquity. One famous patron was Jean Vianney, the Curé of Ars, who was born in France in 1786 and was canonized a saint in 1925. His spiritual fame was so great that during the last year of his life, over one hundred thousand pilgrims spent days waiting outside his church to see and hear him preach. He spent from sixteen to eighteen hours a day hearing confessions. The Curé once confided to a fellow priest: "My friend, here is my recipe: I give them a small penance and the remainder I myself perform in their stead." His ambitious use of the scourge as a means of penance brought him extraordinary psychic powers that he used for the spiritual welfare of his community. Unfortunately, his reputation as a holy man, healer, and miracle worker brought him not only unwanted fame but critical attention by Church officials. The bishop criticized his passion for fasting and extreme discipline, and demanded that he stop torturing himself. Vianney complied, yet he explained: "When I could do with my body what I wanted, God refused me nothing." (*The Curé of Ars* by Fr. Bartholomew O'Brien, Tan Books and Publishers, Inc., 1956, 1987.)

The tradition of self-mortification is certainly not exclusive to medieval mystics. In the Mesoamerica Mayan religion, royalty and priests bled their penises to stimulate visions. In the Aztec religion, warriors practiced autosacrifice, the bleeding of oneself through insertion of spines or other ritual implements, specifically to enhance direct communication with deities.

The physiological dynamics at play are well known. Fasting and ascetic practices such as bloody flagellation are very effective modalities producing brilliant visionary experiences. In prolonged fasting, the body is deprived a significant amount of sugar, which lowers the brain's ability to function effectively. A severe vitamin deficiency enables a decrease in nicotinic acid, which produces visions. Self-mortification has been used as a tool of religious aspirants because it releases a large amount of adrenaline and histamine, which affects consciousness and intensifies the potential of visions. Large quantities of adrenaline can cause hallucinations, and festering wounds — not treated properly — produce toxins that disrupt the enzyme systems controlling brain functions. These toxins are produced by the decomposition of protein that goes directly into the bloodstream. In addition to protracted fasting, long periods without sleep and constraining the body in painful positions also play a part in increasing psychological and physiological stress.

There have always been scholarly critics who have summarily denounced mystics in cruel psychoanalytical terms. Evelyn Underhill called St. Teresa of Ávila "the patron saint of hysterics" and St. Paul "an epileptic." (*Mysticism,* Doubleday, New York, 1990); Eric John Dingwall labeled St. Mary Magdalene de' Pazzi "a masochistic exhibitionist," (*Very Peculiar People: Portrait Studies in the Queer, the Abnormal and the Uncanny* by Eric John Dingwall, Rider and Company, 1950) and W.W. Meissner trivialized St. Ignatius of Loyola, the founder of the Jesuits, as "a phallic narcissistic personality." ("Ignatius of Loyola," *The Psychology of a Saint* by W.W. Meissner, S.J., M.D., Yale University Press, New Haven and London, 1992.)

Dr. Richard von Krafft-Ebing, in his classic work on abnormal sexual pathology, *Psychopathia Sexualis*, called de' Pazzi "a heroine of flagellation." Kraff-Ebing asserted that the whippings de' Pazzi imposed on herself from her earliest youth caused the destruction of her nervous system and invoked massive hallucinations.

The mystical visions brought on by ascetic practices and the positive effect of these visions have been supplanted by modern day denouncements decrying, as Krafft-Ebing did, that these practices "clearly show the significance of flagellation as a sexual excitant." The brilliance of de' Pazzi's mysticism — which I will address shortly — was lost on Krafft-Ebing. The "Grand Mysticism" of two of the greatest figures of their time, St. Teresa of Ávila and St. Catherine of Siena (now criticized as a neurotic anorexic so desperate for attention that she starved herself to death), are all but dismissed.

Why were mystics and holy men and women important to their communities? It would be unconscionable to reduce their significance to two key points; yet, for the task at hand I would confine their "purpose" in the communities they served as follows: They provided prayers for illnesses (and hoped-for miracles in a world without medical care) by, people believed, having established a special relationship with God; and by praying for the souls of the dead. People were very concerned over the fate of their souls.

Modern scholars have elected to ignore the religious practices of the time and deny the positive framework in which the disciplines of mystics were developed. To judge these mystics by modern standards demeans the ecstatic modality they followed. The path they chose was paved and lit, well traveled, and richly fulfilling in spiritual commerce.

I have chosen to briefly showcase the lives of three great mystics: Saint Mary Magdalene de' Pazzi, Saint Margaret Mary Alacoque, and Blessed Henry Suso. They chose a locus to revelation that was drastic and harsh but nevertheless bore luminous fruit. In contrast, the means available to us is both elegantly simple and highly effective: Ayahuasca. Linking medieval mysticism and the modern use of ayahuasca may seem improbable; however, there are striking similarities that, students of shamanism will note, unites these two disciplines.

## Mary Magdalene de' Pazzi

Like most mystics of the Middle Ages, the life of Mary Magdalene de' Pazzi has been judged – in my opinion unfairly – by modern standards that should not be applied to medieval times. Mary Magdalene de' Pazzi (baptized Caterina) was born in Florence, Italy in 1566. Details about her florid mystical life are well known through two biographies written by her confessors: a contemporary life written by a fellow nun and eyewitness testimony given two years after her death during the petition for her beatification. An ascetic and cloistered nun, Mary Magdalene was also very productive, having dictated two books and corresponded with religious leaders and laypersons.

Caterina experienced her first ecstasy at twelve while looking at a sunset. At fourteen, she entered a convent but after fifteen months of ascetic penances her family brought her home. Against her family's wishes, Caterina then entered a Carmelite convent as a novice at the age of seventeen and took the name of Mary Magdalene. She continued her ascetic practices with such eagerness that she became dangerously ill. Upon taking her vows as a nun, Mary Magdalene became enraptured for the next forty days. Her mystical experiences were taken down by two nuns and later published as *The Forty Days*. At the end of forty days of ecstasy, Jesus offered her either a crown of thorns or a crown of flowers. Repeatedly, Mary Magdalene begged for the crown of thorns.

Incredibly, when she was only nineteen, Mary Magdalene received the stigmata, the physical wounds of Jesus' crucifixion. Receiving the stigmata was (and still is) recognized as a sign of immense spiritual favor. Mary Magdalene's physical austerities and mortifications in the service to God dominated her life and rest as the centerpiece of her sanctity.

Mary Magdalene's interior religious life flourished. Not yet twenty, she defiantly told her superiors that God had instructed her to eat only bread and water. Whatever meager food she was compelled by obedience to eat, she vomited. Devils haunted her day and night, tempting her with fragrant food to break her strenuous fasts. Demons would fling open pantry cabinets and offer her delicacies. Because of her rigorous self-mortifications she was reduced to crawling. Bridled with feelings of guilt and considering herself unworthy of the nun's habit, she wore a simple tunic.

She was richly rewarded for her penances by visions of Jesus. Mary Magdalene was widely recognized as having the power of precognition, clairvoyance, and telekinesis. Her power to heal was so extraordinary that her extreme ascetic practices, not mandated by her convent, were tolerated. After her death, the convent used her veil and pillow for their healing properties.

Mary Magdalene's intimate relationship with Jesus is celebrated by the ecstatic words she spoke to Him: "Mine eyes into the eyes of Thy mercy. Mine ears into Thine ears, that they may hear and understand the voice of my Spouse. My mouth into Thy mouth, that my mouth may speak what my Spouse speaks to me. My breast in Thy breast, my Beloved!"

Her devotion to Jesus was so powerful that the word "love" would drive her into ecstasy. She said to Jesus: "I can no longer bear so much love, retain it in Thyself." Her passionate longing for Jesus burned so bright inside her body that Mary Magdalene could not wear woolen garments in the winter. Overcome by this fiery love, Mary Magdalene felt it as an immense and consuming flame that seared inside her. To fight off the demonic temptations that prevailed against her, she would push sharp metal objects into her skin and pour hot wax on her flesh.

Mary Magdalene's intentional life of mortifications and suffering culminated in a last illness that left her emaciated and bedridden, suffering with head and chest pains, continual fevers and constant coughing. Her asceticism had destroyed her health. Paralyzed in her bed, she suffered severe bedsores. Her lifelong motto had been, "To suffer, not to die!" Her body, on which she had inflicted so much pain, lay in this manner for three years. She began to pray for "il nudo patire," a painful death. Mary Magdalene died in 1607 at the age of forty-one. She was canonized a saint in 1669. (*Secrets of a Seraph: The Spiritual Doctrine of Saint Mary Magdalene de' Pazzi, Carmelite and Mystic* by The Rev. Salvator Thor-Salviat, The Carmelite Third Order Press, 1961.)

### Margaret Mary Alacoque

When Margaret Mary was twenty-six years old, she had three evocative revelations that would dramatically alter the course of her life and shepherd into the world the brilliant iconography of the Sacred Heart of Jesus. The first revelation was so provocative that its physical effects dominated Margaret Mary's entire life. The vision that would consume her took place on December 27, 1673.

Jesus appeared to Sister Margaret Mary and pressed her closely to His breast. He demanded Margaret Mary's own heart, which He took from her body and merged into His own. He said to her: "My daughter, I have thy heart and I give thee Mine, that thou mayest forever live in Me." When He returned her heart, it flamed inside her body. The intense suffering she felt was always present. "The pain of this wound," she wrote, "is so precious to me, causes me transports so lively, that it burns me alive, it consumes me."

Margaret Mary's sole desire was to live a life dedicated to suffering. She heroically succeeded in her quest for spiritual perfection through physical pain. She wrote of her ambition: "Suffering alone can render life endurable to me." An ascetic athlete, Margaret Mary began her life as an advocate of suffering at a very early age.

Margaret was born in 1647 in L'Hautecour, Burgurdy, France. On the death of her father, eight-year-old Margaret was sent to a Poor Clares school. When she was ten she returned home, suffering from rheumatic fever. Margaret was to be bedridden for the next five years. It was only when her family made a special vow to the Blessed Virgin that Margaret was cured. This miracle, attributed to the Blessed Virgin's intervention, set the course for Margaret Mary's future.

As a young girl, Margaret sought a small corner of her family's garden as a retreat, and spent days there without eating and drinking, lost in prayer. She began to practice austere mortifications and devoted herself to caring for the poor and sick. After making a vow of chastity, Margaret began to experience rapturous visions of Jesus. Against the wishes of her family, she refused to be married. Finally, in 1671, she entered the Visitation convent at Paray-le-Monial where she spent the rest of her life.

The novice continued to have intense visions of Jesus. "My Divine Master let me see that this was the time of our betrothal, and, like the most ardent of lovers, He made me taste what was sweetest in the sweetness of His love." Margaret Mary insisted on doing all her convent work on her knees. She spent hours kneeling in prayer and meditation and excelled in the use of the discipline. The Mother Superior of her convent said: "If we had not snatched the scourge from her hands, her blood would have never ceased to flow."

Jesus generously rewarded Margaret Mary's ardor by appearing to her and speaking intimately with her. When Jesus told her she was to be His Spouse, she responded by writing a consecration to Him in her own blood. United to Jesus as his chosen spouse, Margaret Mary's enthusiasm for suffering escalated.

She sought every avenue to harshly diminish even the smallest pleasure. She seasoned her already sparse convent food with ashes. She began to deprive herself of anything to drink from Thursday until Saturday of every week. At another time, she spent fifty days without taking any liquids until she was finally forced to drink by her superiors.

Margaret Mary's sought spiritual perfection the only way she could, through mortification. She wrote: "To avenge in some manner on myself the injury I had done Him, I bound this miserable, criminal body with knotted cords, which I drew so tightly that I could hardly breathe or eat. I kept them on so long that they ate into my flesh. It was only by force and at the cost of cruel suffering that I could get them off again. It was the same with the little chains that I clasped around my arms. I could not remove them without tearing off with them pieces of flesh. I slept on planks, or strewed my bed with sharp sticks."

Like most mystics, Margaret Mary fasted strenuously as a means to bring on her visions. Her second revelation occurred in 1674, a year after the first. Jesus appeared to her with His five wounds shining like five Suns. Flames came from His heart piercing her, and all of humanity, with His divine love. He asked two things of her: the first, to receive communion every first Friday of each month; the second, to pray for an hour every week for the sins of men.

The final revelation took place in 1675. Jesus told Margaret Mary to establish a feast day to honor His Sacred Heart. Margaret Mary died on October 17, 1690. Her incorrupt body is on display at the Shrine of St. Margaret Mary in the sanctuary of the Chapel of the Visitation Convent at Paray-le-Monial where the apparitions of the Sacred Heart of Jesus took place. She was canonized a saint in 1920. (*The Life of Saint Margaret Mary Alacoque* by Rt. Rev. Émile Bougaud, Tan Books and Publishers, Inc., 1890, 1920.)

**Henry Suso**

"I have lost myself in God. No one can reach me here." Blessed Henry Suso is acknowledged as one of the three great male mystics of medieval German mysticism, along with fellow Dominicans Meister Eckhart and John Tauler. Suso wrote three influential books, *The Life of the Servant, Little Book of Divine Truth* and *Little Book of Eternal Wisdom. The Life of the Servant* is an autobiographical account of Suso's pious practices, visions, and mystical experiences. Suso described his raptures, luminous experiences of God, and exactly how he went about achieving these states – he spent over sixteen years subjecting his body to excruciating torture. Suso believed, as most mystics did, that "Suffering was part of love."

The litany of Suso's long years punishing his body (he entered religious life when he was thirteen) is spectacularly harrowing. Besides prolonged and cruel fasts (he even severely restricted his intake of water), he wore a hairshirt and an iron chain until he bled "like a fountain and had to give it up." He made an undergarment of hair containing a hundred and fifty pointed brass nails that were sharpened to a fine point. The vermin that lived on his body would suck and bite him. He placed a belt around his neck and attached two rings of leather to support his hands. Every night he spent this way, with his hands and arms raised and painfully stretched. He devised other tortures for his body: He made a wooden cross and hammered thirty iron nails to it and wore the cross under his clothes day and night for eight years.

In the final year of his mortifications Suso added seven needles that caused deep wounds he bore in praise of the Mother of God. In addition, Suso flagellated himself twice a day, driving the nails deep into his flesh so that they remained there for him to pull out. Further, Suso constructed a scourge with sharp thorns and hooks that caused pieces of his flesh to be ripped out.

What drove Suso to such bloodthirsty excess? Suso's rapturous visions began with a supernatural experience. He wrote that his soul was caught up – in the body or out of the body, he knew not – and he saw and heard what tongues could not express. At one point he felt like he was floating in the air. He said: "If this is not heaven, I do not know what heaven is. Enduring all the suffering that one can put into words is not rightly enough to justify one's possessing this eternally." After one hour or more, he felt like a person who had come from another world. Departed souls often appeared to Suso telling him what had happened to them, what their punishment was, and the help they needed.

Suso believed his penitent asceticism was fundamental to his quest for heroic piety. He reached his spiritual goal – full union with the Godhead – when he entered into Spiritual Marriage with Eternal Wisdom. His writings are revered as classics of mysticism, but more importantly, represent an honest first-person account of the spiritual process in action.

## Self Flagellation Today

If flagellation and its use as a paramystical instrument were predominately a medieval fetishism, it would be appropriate to strongly admonish the Catholic Church alone for its past popularity. Yet outside western spirituality the religious practice of self-flagellation and "aberrant self-torture" continues to be sanctioned today.

Cases of similar feats abound in religious communities today and stand as tributes to the powerful agency of religious belief. Modern-day scientists call these abilities the "Deliberately Caused Bodily Damage" (DCBD) phenomenon, whereby individuals cause serious wounds to their bodies without feeling pain, loss of blood, or infection. In these feats, wound healing is usually rapid. The most recognized and studied group is a Sufi school known as Tariqa Casnazaniyyah, an Arabic-Kurdish name that means "the way of the secret that is known to no one."

This sect has followers in many countries including Iraq, Jordan, Sudan, and India. The power of invulnerability to physical damage and harm are transferred from master to student. The present Master of Tariqa Casnazaniyyah, Shaikh Muhammad al-Casnazani, allowed researchers from the Paramann Programme Laboratories in Jordan to study twenty-eight dervishes. The remarkable feats performed by the dervishes do not come about by any meditation or hypnosis. Any male can join the order of Tariqa Casnazaniyyah by declaring his intent and then submitting to a ritual initiation that takes only two or three minutes. The initiation is simply a handshake and reciting a pledge of loyalty to Tariqa Casnazaniyyah. Then the initiate is granted permission to perform feats that demonstrate the spiritual powers of Tariqa Casnazaniyyah.

In the Paramann Laboratories the dervishes were able to insert skewers and spikes into different parts of their body. The instruments used were not sterilized, and, at the request of observers, were deliberately contaminated before inserting them into their bodies. With the aid of hammers, they drove daggers into their skull bones and knives just below their eyes. They held red-hot iron plates with their bare hands and even bit them. And finally, the dervishes chewed and swallowed glass and sharp razor blades causing no harm to the inner tissues of the mouth and organs of the digestive system. Besides DCBD feats, the dervishes are able to exhibit no damaging effects – called Damage Resistance feats – from exposing their bodies to fire and snake handling, and to severe electrical shocks.

Further, the calendar (a respected group of dervishes who are deputies of the Master) can pierce the body of any person. Califas can use the bodies of children, non-dervishes, and even non-Muslims to exhibit their spiritual abilities.

The researchers were unable to identify what methods their subjects used to perform DCBD feats. The researchers concluded: "Given the nature of the applied stimuli, the seriousness of the induced damage, the unusual reactions, and the instantaneous healings observed in DCBD feats, these phenomena reveal immunities and damage repairing abilities that seem far beyond the normal capacities of [the] human body." The researchers made an astonishing statement: "DCBD which demonstrate[s] very unusual healing capabilities could well open a new era in medicine, and consequently, could well be responsible for unprecedented improvement in the welfare of humanity."

To commemorate the martyrdom of their most revered saint, in 1996, nearly 4,000 Shitte Muslim men in Nabatiyeh, Lebanon whipped themselves and slashed their heads in remembrance of the killing of the seventh-century saint Hussein. The men lacerated their heads with curved swords and razors and used iron chains to beat their chests. Blood poured from the shaven heads of elderly men and boys as young as two. Several people fainted from self-inflicted wounds in the four-hour ritual, but no deaths were reported. Similar ceremonies involving thousands of other men took place elsewhere in Lebanon. (For a discussion of DCBD, I recommend "Healing By Altered States of Consciousness: Science of Trance or Science in Trance?" by Jamal N. Hussein, Louray J. Fatoohi, Shetha Al-Dargarzelli, Nadja Almukhtar.)

**Mysticism Defined**

In *The Psychology of Religious Mysticism*, James H. Leuba defines "mystical" as "Any experience taken by the experiencer to be a contact (not through the senses, but "immediate," "intuitive') or union of the self with a larger-than-self, be it called the World-Spirit, God, the Absolute, or otherwise." Leuba also defines mysticism in the context of Protestantism: "Mysticism is a deification of man," it is "a merging of the individual will with the Divine," "an intuitive certainty of contact with the Divine." The author concludes: "In this view, whatever tends to sharpen the demarcation between the self and the not-self, whatever leads to an isolation of the subject from the Principle of Life, is anti-mystical."

I have chosen Leuba's definition since his well-regarded work primarily deals with Christian mysticism, yet he acknowledges the diverse paths taken by other religious systems to enter into an ecstatic relationship with God. He concedes that there are diverse methods to experience God, such as the Ghost-Dance religion of the American

Indians, the Sufis' dancing dervishes, and the use of certain plants by primitive cultures.

Interestingly, Leuba, like most religious scholars, is no fan of mysticism. While admitting that states of ecstatic intoxication exist, he unfairly attributes the ecstasy of mystics to unintentional bouts of orgasm. Of Margaret Mary Alacoque, Leuba writes: "Her case is clearly one of erotomania."

There are unique bodily sensations associated with extreme mortification, willful self-starvation, as well as ingesting ayahuasca. But none of these states can be confused with orgasm. I have never read of anyone experiencing orgasm as revelatory and life-changing. Orgasm is also not known as an agent for visions or for lasting two to three hours. After experiencing ayahuasca visions and the intense physical sensations that accompany it, I would never confuse the two, even metaphorically. To say these "unsophisticated" nuns and priests experienced orgasm is just too simplistic and naïve. How could the raptures of St. Teresa of Ávila – that literally caused her to levitate – be termed orgiastic? If there is a correlation, then we must reevaluate our sexual experiences. We are all missing something.

**Ayahuasca as a Spiritual Conduit**

I propose that the negative aspects of ingesting ayahuasca – the purging, diarrhea, and nausea commonly experienced as well as the dietary and sexual restrictions – are a form of mortification *for Westerners*. It is therefore appropriate to compare it to the practices of the mystics and saints of the Middle Ages. The outcome accomplished by both disciplines can be illuminating, revelatory, and extraordinary. But there is one significant difference: ayahuasca does not destroy the body.

In "The Ayahuasca Phenomenon: Jungle Pilgrims: North Americans Participating in Amazon Ayahuasca Ceremonies" by Kim Kristensen, the author quotes David Maybury-Lewis saying: "If drinking yage (ayahuasca) is so unpleasant and frightening, why do people persist in using it? Because they believe the terror is something a person must overcome in order to attain knowledge."

It is regrettable that those who have never had a mystical experience themselves often choose to scrutinize the mysticism of others. This is a major flaw that must be taken into account when considering the authenticity and truth of mystical experiences as evaluated by scholars.

**Demonic Attacks and Serpent Imagery in Ayahuasca**

Demonic attacks, considered ridiculous in our culture, are very much a reality in Peru. I was surprised at the seriousness in which this concept is regarded. Religious writers consider demonic attacks and possession, hallmarks in the lives of mystics and saints, as archaic as religious flagellation. This is a narrow, culture-bound view. Throughout the history of religion, mystics are savagely tormented by demons. For the curanderos, reality is populated with good and evil spirits. People can be physically harmed by bruijos and evil spirits; these attacks are not psychological manifestations of a troubled mind.

The lives of mystics are replete with fantastic tales of demonic attacks that are now believed to be an unfortunate byproduct of psychotic personalities crippled by sexual deviancy and crazed by starvation and cruel self-torture. Here is one such example from *Holy Anorexia* by Rudolph Bell (The University of Chicago Press, 1985): "Snakes, toads, and ferocious beasts abound in the hallucinations of holy anorexics, but why assume that these have sexual as well as religious significance? When St. Francesca de' Ponziani (d. 1440) saw a serpent she believed the Devil was attacking her, and it seems not to be of historical consequence that this serpent may have symbolized repressed penis envy."

In *The Life of Antony*, Athanasius describes a "commonplace" demonic attack on St. Antony (d. 356), who is recognized as one of the founders of Christian monasticism: "The demons, as if breaking through the building's four walls, and seeming to enter through them, were changed into the forms of beasts and reptiles. The place immediately was filled with the appearance of lions, bears, leopards, bulls, and serpents, asps, scorpions and wolves, and each of these moved in accordance with its form."

It is impossible to review any literature on ayahuasca without coming across the image of the serpent. However terrifying it appears to us, Westerners are advised not to be afraid of the snakes, serpents, and other horrific animals that inhabit ayahuasca visions. Religious scholars would be shocked at Jeremy Narby's statement in *The Cosmic Serpent. DNA and the Origins of Knowledge* (Jeremy P. Tarcher/Putnam, 1999): "Then I learned that in an endless number of myths, a gigantic and terrifying serpent, or a dragon, guards the axis of knowledge, which is represented in the form of a ladder (or a vine, a cord, a tree…). I also learned that (cosmic) serpents abound in the creation myths of the world and that they are not only at the origin of knowledge, but of life itself."

The serpent imagery that frightened a past culture is embraced as revelatory by another and dismissed as mythical (or denounced as Freudian "penis envy") by our own.

### The Shamanic Diet and Religious Fasting

There are demonstrative similarities between the stringent practices of saints and mystics and ayahuasquero initiates. The process of becoming an ayahuasca shaman is arduous and involves years of commitment to celibacy, solitude, cultural mortifications, and extreme fasting.

In an informative interview, ayahuasquero Don Agustin Rivas-Vasquez discussed his six-year shamanic apprenticeship with Jaya Bear (*Shaman's Drum*, No. 44, Mar/May 1997). Don Agustin spent a year living in solitude in a tree. Regarding his initiatory diet, he said: "For a year, I ate only rice and plantains. I didn't eat any meat, butter, fruit, sugar, or salt. I learned many things over that year, by dieting and working with different plants."

Food asceticism was an important feature in the lives of mystics and saints. Like Don Agustin, they abstained from using salt, sugar, and spices and never ate meat, fruit, or fish.

The role fasting has played in the history of nearly all religions cannot be disputed. In The Gospel According to Mark (9:24-28), Jesus' disciples are unable to rid a man of an unclean spirit. Jesus is summoned and commands the unclean spirit to leave the man. Later, his disciples ask him why they were not able to cast out the spirit. "And he said to them, 'This kind can be cast out in no way except by prayer and fasting.'" Jesus identifies fasting as a powerful instrument – a tool his apostles did not, or were not willing, to use. The words of

Jesus were not lost on the men and women of the Middle Ages who sought mystical union with God. Coupled with prayer and physical mortifications, the spiritual graces of long, ascetic fasting were well known.

Fundamentally, a question arises: "Does unintentional starvation produce visions?" I am not aware of any research that has addressed this. The obvious inappropriate nature of this query – no one would be so insensitive to poll survivors of Nazi concentration camps or famine victims – leaves this entire topic open to conjecture. Further, there are strict protocols that would prohibit such research being undertaken.

My interest in the relationship between self-starvation and visions led me to conduct a one-year pilot questionnaire of self-described anorexics called "The Religious and Spiritual Aspects of Anorexia Nervosa." Over 1,250 anorexics responded to the detailed questionnaire that aimed to see if there is a correlation between self-starvation and religious experiences. The raw data I collected requires statistical analysis. I have contacted several anorexia nervosa organizations regarding this questionnaire but to no avail. Anorexia afflicts mostly upper-middle class families. With residential treatment easily costing $50,000 – and the success rate unknown – the medical community is more interested in years of therapy and treatment rather than solutions.

Nonetheless I can firmly state that intentionality plays a primary role. A mystic not only fasted, but prayed.

In *The Doors of Perception, Heaven and Hell*, Aldous Huxley commented on the role of fasting in visionary states: "A person under the influence of mescaline or lysergic acid will stop seeing visions when given a large dose of nicotinic acid. This helps to explain the effectiveness of fasting as an inducer of visionary experience. By reducing the amount of available sugar, fasting lowers the brain's biological efficiency and so makes possible the entry into consciousness of material possessing no survival value."

Piero Camporesi, author of *The Incorruptible Flesh: Bodily Mutation and Mortification in Religion and Folklore* (Cambridge University Press, 1988), acknowledges the potency of fasting: "…the efficacy of fasting for the purposes of producing a visionary experience cannot be underestimated, or of restricted diets in unleashing hallucinatory 'highs' in a controlled and secret environment. The combination of cell and fasting was a melting pot for the visionary experience."

## SpiritQuest

Thirty days before my arrival at the SpiritQuest retreat, which is located along the banks of the Rio Momón outside Iquitos, Peru, I began an exacting interpretation of the recommended "Shamanic Diet." I took my lifelong, restrictive 500 calories per day diet and further eliminated all salt, sugar, oils, and spices. On the evening of Dec. 29, 2000, I was confident I had prepared myself and was ready – at least physically – to participate in my first ayahuasca ceremony.

Later I asked Howard Lawler, founder of SpiritQuest, why my experiences with ayahuasca were more brilliant in scope than the other eight drinkers. Howard said my exact adherence to the diet was the significant factor. I was the only participant to do so. I also attribute my Amazonian well being to my strict diet. Seven out of the ten participants at SpiritQuest spent nearly half of our 11-day ayahuasca journey sick with various infirmities and were often bedridden. I did not have any nausea or the dreaded diarrhea that most foreigners fear and often experience. Clearly, the importance of following the dietary restrictions (as well as sexual abstinence) is well documented in the literature on ayahuasca.

I should mention that a few people in my group experienced nausea and vomiting but no visions whatsoever. Subsequently, during other ceremonies they chose to try inducing visions by drinking more than one cup of ayahuasca. One woman, despite two cups of ayahuasca, still did not have the visionary experiences she sought. This clearly defies a physiological explanation.

The religious significance of sexual abstinence need not be discussed here; however, I would like to briefly mention the sexual restrictions recommended during an ayahuasca retreat at SpiritQuest. We were told not to engage in any sexual activity three days prior to taking ayahuasca, while at the retreat, and three days afterwards. During the retreat I asked why and was told: "The Goddess Ayahuasca is very jealous." I did not question this because I went to Peru to fully engage in and respect the religious nature of the experience, not to circumvent any ritual. I told my husband I intended not to challenge the Goddess Ayahuasca on this.

I have been asked if the dietary restrictions are solely for the protection of novices and do not apply to curanderos, shamanic adepts, and long-term users of ayahuasca. The highly restrictive "shamanic diet" does facilitate the visionary aspect of the experience. The scientific data unequivocally supports this statement. (For a more complete evaluation of the data, see *The Biology of Human Starvation* by A. Keys, University of Minnesota Press, 1950.)

Whether dietary and sexual restrictions are psychological in nature and merely ceremonial is unimportant. The value of ritual and its primary function is to prepare the individual for a spiritual transformation.

## Bigu: An Unrecognized Factor in Mysticism and Curanderismo?

Many mystics and saints did die of willful self-starvation and severe mortification practices. However, I would like to suggest an alternative to the concept of enforced fasting. There may be another state attained that allows some mystics and shamans to work unencumbered by the effects of starvation.

Qigong is an ancient Chinese healing art that consists of gentle movements with deep breathing, self-massage, and meditation. An unusual byproduct of Qigong is a state called "Bigu," in which practitioners experience a complete loss of hunger. Practitioners do not take any food and need only drink some water or beverage. There is no sense of hunger in the Bigu state. Practitioners feel full and are actually uncomfortable if they drink or eat. If they do eat, vomiting may occur. Most say the state makes them more alert and provides them with increased energy. Practitioners maintain they are able to conduct normal activities without any harmful effects.

In 1988, Chinese researchers studied a thirteen-year-old girl who had experienced Bigu for three hundred days. According to the report, the girl said she had avoided eating for more than four years. The researchers found that despite the girl's severe lack of caloric and nutritional intake, she responded well to physical activities and maintained a normal life.

Ancient Chinese texts describe Bigu as important for the well being of the human body and as a cure for some diseases. Bigu is not considered fasting or imposed starvation, since it occurs unintentionally. It is a state of being that is said to correspond to one's moral attitudes. It is theorized that in a state of Bigu, "the human body may be able to absorb enough unknown elements and high quality energies other than oxygen, hydrogen, nitrogen, solar energy from the atmosphere and synthesize them into body calories and nutrition."

In 1992, U.S. researchers studied four persons who had experienced Bigu for several months. The subjects, who had practiced Yan Xin Qigong, were observed and closely monitored for 30 days. The study's purpose was to evaluate the physiological and psychological functions of Bigu on the body. The results of the study proved remarkable. Most subjects lost some weight and had low body temperatures, blood pressures, and pulse rates. The biochemical and hematological indices were within the normal range. The subjects were able to maintain their lifestyles and in some cases, improve their aptitude test scores. The study was not able to explain the phenomenon of Bigu.

In June 2000, the First National Conference on the Bigu Manifestation was hosted by my friends Rustum Roy (as Conference Chair) and Gary Schwartz (who organized the 1992 U.S. bigu study). While the Bigu phenomenon entails the cessation of eating solid food for periods of weeks to months and even years, while maintaining a normal daily life, the researchers concluded that the bigu state is "a 'mind-body' balanced state that requires only 250-300 calories or even less, instead of the usual 2,000 calories, to run the human engine for a day." Both Roy and Schwartz insist I am in a "spontaneous" state of bigu and this, they reasoned, may be the cause of the potency of my ayahuasca visions. (For a comprehensive review of Bigu, see "Four Cases of Qigong-related Bigu: A Challenge for Nutritional Science and Energy Medicine" by Yan Xin, Raymond Lee, Xutian Wu, S.M. Wu and Gary E. R. Schwartz, *Alternative Therapies in Health and Medicine*, submitted May 22, 1997.)

The lifelong dietary practices of ayahuasca shamans have yet to be studied. What has been studied, and ignored, is the explanation mystics give for their diets. Their own words are dismissed. Margaret Ebner (1291-1351) was a Dominican nun and mystic who wrote about her mystical union with Christ in *The Revelations of Margaret Ebner*. After experiencing an "indescribably mysterious lightness of body," she wrote: "From that moment I never felt any desire for bodily food, no matter how long I waited to eat." Interestingly, Margaret also felt the need to give up sugar: "And I had the desire to give up all sweet things for the sake of the sweetness I received from God."

St. Catherine of Siena, one of the greatest mystics of the Catholic Church (and now anointed anorexia's poster child), had a life filled with brilliant visions and extraordinary mystical experiences, which were highlighted by her Mystical Marriage to Jesus and stigmata. In one vision Jesus asked her to drink from his side wound. Thereafter, she refused all food, living solely on the sacrament of the Holy Eucharist. Catherine was twenty-five years old at that time and following that vision did not eat anything for the remaining eight years of her life. She also slept only a half an hour a day. Her ability to survive exclusively on the Eucharist caused a sensation in her religious community. Her confessors demanded she eat; but even a small amount of food caused her to vomit. If any food reached her stomach, her face swelled and became disfigured. Eventually, she refused to even attempt to eat.

Catherine herself said she wanted to eat, but she could not. She said she was following God's will. For the last eight years of her life, Catherine's inability to eat (called *inedia*) was miraculous and not an intentional act of self-discipline. Moreover, it was often thought in medieval times that the inability to eat was a sign of demonic possession, a charge a nun like Catherine – with the Inquisition at hand – would not actively promote. On January 1, 1380, as Catherine contemplated the Feast of the Circumcision, she decided to increase her ascetic practices by not drinking any water. She certainly understood the effect it would have on her body. After a month she was severely dehydrated and in debilitating physical anguish. She died on April 29, 1380. Catherine never told anyone why she decided on this course of self-denial, and scholars have summarily condemned it as simply the product of severe depression.

**Bitter Herbs**

The vile, lingering bitter taste of ayahuasca is a defining hallmark of the experience. The bitter taste accompanying many herbs possessing hallucinatory qualities is well documented. Medieval people were familiar with the hallucinatory properties of certain herbs, such as the thorn apple.

Did mystics use commonly found hallucinogenic herbs to enable them to have religious visions? Some modern writers have taken this position. Certainly the local townspeople and religious authorities would have known if this were the case. The selfless lives of mystics and the good works they provided their communities is what ultimately made them revered and honored as living saints. It was not their personal visions but their miraculous healings and prayers that proved to be of value to others. However, students of herbaria will find the following of much interest and offers fascinating conjecture.

The plain, coarse convent food was deemed too rich for St. Margaret Mary Alacoque, so "she seasoned it with ashes to render it more unpalatable. She deprived herself of every kind of beverage; and at one time she took the resolution not to drink anything from Thursday until Saturday of every week." In *The Life of Blessed Birgitta of Sweden: Life and Selected Revelation* (Paulist Press, 1990), we are told that every Friday, Birgitta (d.1373), in honor of Christ's passion on the cross, held "in her mouth a certain very bitter herb, which is called *genicana*. She also did this on other days when she had uttered some unconsidered or incautious word." The life of Sicilian Eustochia of Messina (d.1485) was that of a classic mystic: a meager bread crumbs-and-water diet, flagellation, wearing of a hairshirt, and praiseworthy work with the poor and sick. She is said to have "always added bitter white herbs to all her food." (*Holy Anorexia* by Rudolph M. Bell, The University of Chicago Press, 1985.)

During his life Suso (d. 1663) "abstained from bread for five years, from wine for ten years, and ate only herbs, dried fruits and beans, to which he added a powder, which several religious who tasted it described as of unspeakable bitterness. The vegetables which he ate on Fridays were of such repugnant savor that a friar, who tasted them with the tip of his tongue, was so sickened that for several days all food caused him nausea." Piero Camporesi identifies the powder Suso used as "the bitterest wormwood." Moreover, in Camporesi's translation, Suso's Friday food was not "vegetables" but "a particular herb, which was so bitter…"

St. Catherine of Siena also used an unidentified herb; however, no one reading about her life would conclude it was anything but a "bitter herb." Her biographer, Raymond of Capua, in *The Life of Catherine of Siena* (Michael Glazier, Inc., Wilmington, Delaware 1980), wrote: "She made it her practice, therefore, not to swallow such herbs as she put into her mouth, but only to chew them and then expel the solid matter from her mouth."

St. Catherine of Genoa in her mystical work *The Spiritual Dialogue* wrote: "[God] made her moderate in her eating so that she stopped eating fruit (of which she was very fond) or meat or anything rich. So that she would still further lose the taste for eating, He had her use hepatic oil and ground agracio, with which she would season any food she had a particular liking for." One modern writer speculates that "agracio" is a mistranslation for "agaric." This invites an entirely new interpretation. Considering Catherine's fame and the sanctity she was well known for – as well as the Church's close watch on those who were revered for their holiness – her intentional use of a hallucinogenic herb as a visionary agent seems incongruous.

The medieval Church viewed "living saints" as problematic. The cult of the saint took people away from God and Jesus and undermined Church authority. "Living saints" were carefully monitored for fear they preached something contrary to doctrine. They interfered with the priesthood's role as intermediary between man and God. While the Church could not stop people's devotion and need for "living saints," they certainly kept abreast of their visionary and mystical forays. Clark Heinrich, author of *Strange Fruit: Alchemy, Religion and Magical Foods: A Speculative History* (Bloomsberry Publishing, London 1995), proposes that fly agaric was the agent for the visions of Abraham, Moses, and even Jesus.

## Purges and Vomitory Practices of the Middle Ages

The evacuatory and vomitory nature of ayahuasca is well known. What is of interest here is the belief held in the Middle Ages regarding the healing properties of these practices. At the time, vomiting and induced evacuative remedies were seen as the chief measures for ensuring a healthy and long life.

Is there indeed a value to the side effects that ingesting ayahuasca facilitates?

During the Middle Ages white hellebore or veratrum, which was called a "sacred medicine," and black hellebore (the most drastic) were deemed sovereign treatments for cleansing the body and liberating the soul. Piero Camporesi has this to say about such practices: "The ravaging effects of the hellebore, the hastening and slowing of the pulse, nervous system and brain, caused by veratrum, the fainting fits and therapeutic convulsions, the leaps into unreality, the loss of balance (to which should be added other kinds of permanent toxification cause by other herbs and self-punitory diets) may have had some imponderable relationships (though small and not verifiable) with the swoonings, catalepsy, warblings and flights of the armies of ecstatics, convulsionary visionaries, in that atmosphere charged with giddiness, raptures and loss of consciousness."

Camporesi is obviously not a champion of purification rites. He notes that the liberation by purge using the hellebore began with a whole series of preliminary steps including lotions, baths to induce sweating, moistening of the body, poultices, enemas, fomentations, and special diets. Medieval patients were required to undergo a series of emetics and vigorous purges, some lasting for seven days or more, to expel their demons.

Anyone who has taken ayahuasca in a ritual setting can see the similarities. Ayahuasca shamans, like medieval exorcists, may be utilizing the curative aspects of evacuatory and vomitory disciplines in conjunction with the medicine. Perhaps the use of ayahuasca is less drastic, though it's interesting to note that most ayahuasca retreats are usually seven-to-ten days in duration. "The nausea and vomiting that often occur after drinking ayahuasca are probably due to increasing levels of serotonin in the brain, which results in excessive stimulation of the vagus nerve." ("Phytochemistry and Neuropharmacology of Ayahuasca" by Jace C. Calaway, Ph.D., in *Ayahuasca: Hallucinogens, Consciousness, and the Spirit of Nature* edited by Ralph Metzner, Thunder's Mouth Press, New York, 1999.)

## The Healing Power of Saliva

Like Jesus (Mark 7:32-35, 8:22-24 and John 9:6-7), shamans such as Don Agustin use their saliva as a healing agent. This "magical phlegm" is called yachai, and shamans apply it as a healing salve that is spat directly on the diseased part of a patient's body. They also suck the yachai back into themselves. This is certainly not considered repugnant or bizarre behavior. Saints also used their saliva for healing, though modern scholars have cruelly eviscerated its meaning: The mystics were either sensational masochists or their behavior was homoerotic in coloration.

Saint Mary Magdalene de' Pazzi frequently healed her sisters of leprosy and skin diseases by licking their sores. She even sucked the wound of one sister who was suffering from a leg ulcer that had festered with maggots. Saint Catherine of Siena worked with the dying during an outbreak of the plague in her city. She assisted diseased patients using her mouth to clean the putrefying breast of an ill woman. Saint Margaret Mary Alacoque said she delighted in kissing the wounds of the sick she ministered to. She pressed her lips to the most revolting ulcers and sucked the festering toes of the sick. In her *Mémoire*, Margaret Mary tells of nursing a fellow nun who was dying of stomach cancer by clearing away the sister's vomit with her lips and tongue.

St. Hugh of London (d. 1200), when asked why he kissed a leper replied: "…the leper's kiss cleansed my soul." (*Miracles and the Medieval Mind* by Benedicta Ward, University of Pennsylvania Press, 1982.) Medieval mystics Lukardis of Oberweimar (d. 1309) and Margaret of Faenza (d. 1330) breathed deeply into their fellow nuns' mouths as a means of healing them. The intense physical sensations Lukardis and Margaret said they felt throughout their body they interpreted as receiving of God's grace. Colette of Corbie (d. 1447), who began her religious life as a hermit and later reformed and founded many convents, miraculously multiplied food and wine for her monasteries. She affected cures with food, putting bread she had chewed into the mouths of two sick sisters. On another occasion, her kiss healed a leper. Today, scholars consider these acts "erotic kisses" and have not associated them with traditional shamanic healing practices.

It is my position that mystics such as Catherine of Siena, Mary Magdalene de' Pazzi, and Mary Margaret Alacoque understood the potent healing power of their saliva; they were not, as modern scholars suggest, acting out lesbian desires.

Mata Amritanandamayi, a Hindu holy woman considered a "living saint," transfers her spiritual energy through kisses and hugs. It is said she has hugged nearly a million people. Ammachi also uses her saliva to heal. (*Amma: Healing the Heart of the World* by Judith Cornell, Morrow, William & Co., 2001.)

As we open the door to understanding the significance of the "magical phlegm" of shamans, I hope writers will once again look – perhaps less critically – at the healing practices of medieval saints. (For a discussion of the medicinal value of saliva see *Honey, Mud, Maggots, and Other Medical Marvels: The Science Behind Folk Remedies and Old Wives' Tales* by Robert and Michèle Root-Bernstein, Houghton Mifflin Company, 1997.)

**"There is no language for this"**

In Evelyn Underhill's classic work *Mysticism*, in the chapter titled "Ecstasy and Rapture," she writes: "During the trance, breathing and circulation are depressed. The body is more or less cold and rigid, remaining in the exact position which it occupied at the oncoming of the ecstasy, however difficult and unnatural this pose may be. Sometimes entrancement is so deep that there is complete anaesthesia . . ." And so it was with ayahuasca.

I approached my first ayahuasca ceremony with fear and excitement. I was saying the rosary. Before I drank, I said aloud: Jesus help me. Looking back now, it was gentle preparation for the ceremonies to come. I was able to observe the medicine's effect on me both physically and mentally. The serpent imagery appeared, but it was not terrifying, just marvelous and interesting. I was not prepared – nor were the other first-time drinkers – for how ayahuasca made one feel so very cold. It recalled to me the words of St. Teresa of Ávila: "In these raptures the soul seems no longer to animate the body, and thus the natural heat of the body is felt to be very sensibly diminished: it gradually becomes colder, though conscious of the greatest sweetness and delight. No means of resistance is possible, whereas in union, where we are on our own ground, such a means exists: resistance may be painful and violent but it can almost always be effected." Anyone who has experienced ayahuasca can relate to St. Teresa's words.

For me, the vomiting was necessary to revelation. Ayahuasca told me: "If you want to have visions, this is what you must do." By subjecting myself to the painful physical aspects of ingesting ayahuasca, I was participating in a ritual that was ancient. The medicine accepted me. This was an essential aspect of my personal journey.

Another ceremony was breathtakingly revelatory, as I was shown the world the way it really is. It didn't matter whether I opened or closed my eyes. I vividly experienced what I now call "The Structure of Everything." I also went to a room filled with three-dimensional mathematical equations and ideas. All the knowledge there was assessable. I was reminded of the statement of St. Francesca de' Ponziani (1384-1440) who spoke of being "transported in spirit to a vast place full of remarkable treasures…" During another ecstasy, as she passed from one light to another she entered into what she described as a "splendid hall."

Dr. Raymond Moody, author of several books on near-death experiences including the seminal *Life After Life*, told me he is very familiar with this "room." Under quite different circumstances he has been to this room, which he says appears in many near-death accounts.

In quick succession I asked to be shown an alien world (I entered its "DNA") and then I went into the being of a female spirit, who told me her name was Lady Chen. Finally, I asked for and saw The Face of God.

My experience recalls the reply of the ecstatic levitating saint, Joseph of Copertino when asked "What do mystics see in their ecstasies?" he said: "They find themselves in a great gallery of beautiful things, and in a resplendent mirror hanging therein they see with one glance the wandering essence of all these things, that is, of the arcane mysteries which God is pleased to reveal to them in that superb vision." (*St. Joseph of Copertino* by Fr. Angelo Pastrovicchi, O.M.C., Tan Books and Publishers, Inc., Rockford, IL, 1918, 1990.)

One drinker – in the parlance of the 1970s – appeared to "flip out." Everyone present heard a tremendous crash when Tom Barber lost control of his body and fell from his seat to the floor. Attendants rushed to his aid. I realized, as I watched the "drama" unfold, I would now see the skill of our curanderos in action. Later, both curanderos praised Tom's experience as a "soul flight," though acknowledging Tom was inexperienced and unable to handle his reentry journey without their guidance. At no time did they feel Tom was in any danger. However, it made a stunning impression on all of us: Don't try this at home. Tom Barber, 32 years old in 2000, was a dancer with the Memphis Ballet.

Tom commented further on the onset of his dramatic experience, which he has given me permission to relate: "My body was at this time let loosed of physical concern and toppled from the rocker recliner to the floor of wood planking in what must have been quite a commotion. Seemingly personifying helpless vulnerability, movements became as involuntary as a twitch while dreaming. My body both undulated harmoniously with the icaros and floundered in epileptic-like surges. Consciously aware, though lacking understanding, I felt hands touching me. Whispy sounds of a chacapa came close-by and I recognized don Romulo's songs. Feeling now somewhat possessed, I sensed that an energy at my core was being tantalized by don Romulo's work. It was my first realization that someone was coming to my aid as I slipped through the window of everyday human reality into non-ordinary realms." Tom recovered after several hours of "soul flight" and was in an exceptionally good mood the following morning. He fearlessly participated in all of the ceremonies and said he looked forward to his next SpiritQuest retreat.

Another ceremony centered on healing since one of the participants was quite ill. Tess Bohr, who had left a Kentucky hospital's emergency room to board her plane to Iquitos, was placed in the middle of the room and the curanderos worked on removing the illnesses from her body. I saw, with my eyes open, an Indian man brought forth by the singing of Maestro don Romulo. I was told this genio (spirit doctor) only works with don Romulo. As confirmation of the reality of my "vision," Ken Rolan, another member of the group, also described don Romulo's spirit doctor exactly as I did. We both saw, with our eyes open, his rhythmic dance.

My last ayahuasca ceremony still had hours to go, but after three hours I was able to turn to my husband and tell him I wanted to go to our room. I would leave before each drinker was individually sung to, prayed over, and blessed by Maestro don Romulo and Hermana Mari. The intense visions were subsiding and I felt I could leave the room with my husband's assistance. The icaros were so powerful – does it mean anything if I say the singing was even more intense than the ayahuasca? – and I was anxious to lie down and let the medicine slowly bring me back. Before I drank, I had boldly asked: "Show me the power of Ayahuasca." I do not have the words to describe the experience elegantly yet, though the only word that expresses it is PROFOUND. Ayahuasca showed me why it is revered as a sacred instrument of revelation.

My last ayahuasca ceremony has left me with great sympathy for the task mystics had in confining an indescribable experience to words. They were compelled, by their vow of obedience, to relate their experiences for the inspiration of others. I have chosen, at least for the present, to keep my experience to myself. So far, Jeremy Narby seems to be on the right track in explaining the process in *The Cosmic Serpent: DNA and the Origins of Knowledge*: "People use different techniques in different places to gain access to knowledge of the vital principle. In their visions shamans manage to take their consciousness down to the molecular level."

I suddenly entered and became part of The Web of the World. I will only relate the physical impact of ayahuasca during those two hours. At dinner in Las Vegas with my good friend, James Whinnery, we discussed the comparison of my experience with the loss of consciousness resulting from g-forces that occur in pilots flying fighter aircraft. I likened it to being totally conscious during the g-force state.

Dr. James Whinnery is an expert on g-force-induced loss of consciousness (called g-LOC). I have watched videotapes of Jim's experiments. Many of the pilots Jim worked with reported the sensation of floating above their bodies before losing consciousness. They vividly described sensations that reminded Jim of reports of near-death experiences (NDEs). I told Jim about the physical effects I had experienced with ayahuasca: my mouth hung up, I was slumped in my chair, I completely lost the ability to move, and I was very cold. I had the intense feeling of traveling at a high speed in a swirling motion I could not control.

Jim explained the physiological effects he and his fighter pilots experienced. Blood flow was altered to their brains during head-to-foot acceleration. As full consciousness is lost there is loss of the body's motor function that provides for movement of the muscles. As the muscles relax, the mouth falls open, the neck, arms, torso, and legs also relax, and one becomes completely immobilized. The loss of blood flow to the extremities produces the cold feeling. Jim said these were all conditions pilots experienced during g-force-induced loss of consciousness experiments, as well as loss of bodily functions and control, nausea, and vomiting.

In *The Life of Teresa of Jesus: The Autobiography of Teresa of Ávila*, St. Teresa describes a rapturous experience in this way: "Occasionally I have been able to make some resistance, but at the cost of great exhaustion, for I would feel as weary afterwards as though I had been fighting with a powerful giant. At other times, resistance has been impossible: my soul has been borne away, and indeed as a rule my head also, without my being able to prevent it: sometimes my whole body has been affected, to the point of being raised up from the ground."

Similarly, I felt like I was submerged and absorbed into a g-force induced state of consciousness during my ayahuasca experience very much like the fighter pilots' experience when they exceed their tolerance to g-forces. I felt I had a comparative, harrowing ride without climbing into a centrifuge. I survived being plunged into, enveloped, and engulfed by The Web of the World without losing consciousness.

In a subsequent dinner conversation with Jim, he raised the possibility that ayahuasca may stimulate the vagus nerve, the tenth cranial nerve. The infamous vagus nerve has been suggested as the physical basis for the Kundalini experience (*The Mysterious Kundalini* by Vasant G. Rele, D.B. Taraporevala Sons & Co., Bombay, 1960), and has recently been the subject of intense scientific research.

The electrical stimulation of the vagus nerve is being studied (and now approved by the FDA) as a treatment for depression, diabetes, epilepsy, obesity, and Alzheimer's.

In my personal experience the most important feature of ayahuasca is its ability to render profound visions and revelation without altering one's consciousness in any way. I am an ayahuasca novitiate, but I can firmly attest that I was not in an "altered" state of consciousness. I was in a "heightened" state of consciousness.

## The Ayahuasca Journey at Spiritquest

SpiritQuest was founded by enthnobiologist Howard Lawler in 1997. The goal of SpiritQuest is not only to bring people to the ayahuasca experience under the guidance of skillful curanderos, but also to assist and support the neighboring indigenous Amazonian communities of the Bora and Yahua Indians. SpiritQuest workshops can accommodate up to twelve people, which guarantees that attendees receive personal attention. Lawler has also set up a cooperative food and supply store in the Bora village of San Andres, which is entirely village owned and operated. He has other projects pending for the Yahua community that include a solar water purification system, a village pharmacy, and a women's medicinal plant cultivation project. The goals are geared to community enfranchisement in health, wellness, nutrition, and small enterprises that enable the people to progress in basic quality of life through their own initiative while nurturing cultural preservation and dignity.

At the first retreat I attended in 2000, SpiritQuest was working with two curanderos, Maestro don Romulo and Hermana Mari, recently retired. Maestro ayahuasquero don Romulo was given ayahuasca by his father, a master shaman, when he was eight years old. By the time he was twenty, he was fully initiated in the path of the ayahuasquero and curandero. Don Romulo, who has taken ayahuasca thousands of times, cultivates the ayahuasca and chacruna used in SpiritQuest ceremonies. He lives alone, tending his plantation in the jungle more than four hours distance by boat from Iquitos. Maestro don Romulo has practiced curanderismo for more than forty years.

When I asked don Romulo about his relationship with ayahuasca, he said: "What you need to know about ayahuasca is that there are many things to learn, and many things to see. There are many medicines to be found along the path. This has the power to heal everything that's bad in a person, especially disease. Because Doctor Ayahuasca tells us what the disease or what the problem is with the person and what causes the problem. In many cases it's witchcraft or some bad intention or something generated by the bad intention or the will of others. When I can find out what it is and who did it, I can take it out."

Hermana Mari was born in Lamas in the department of San Martin. She spent her youth in a very remote, rural village in the higher jungle. Hermana Mari has a neighborhood practice in Iquitos and conducts ayahuasca ceremonies twice a week. Her monthly SpiritQuest retreats are the only work she does outside her culture. Her grandfather and grandmother worked with enchanted stones. Her father was a camalongero (a shaman who specializes in the use of camalonga) and did not use ayahuasca.

In an interview I conducted with Hermana Mari, I asked her about her neighborhood practice. "If there are people who are gravely ill," she said, "I will work any day. Whatever day is needed for the healing I'll work, but my scheduled healing ceremonies for the local people are Tuesday and Friday nights. Primarily, people come to me for healing. Often people come to me seeking healing from a witching spell that has been cast. 'Chullachaki' is the king of the mountain and a very good doctor to take out witchcraft. He's a very small elf that has one big foot and one small foot. There is a chullachaki tree that is used as an aphrodisiac for men, as well as treatment for arthritis, rheumatism, and intestinal infections. It's also effective for treating AIDS. Men who have potency problems can alleviate this by drinking a brew made from the chullachaki tree. Here in the forest we have all kinds of medicines for men and for women. The thing I see the most is daño [witchcraft]."

While at SpiritQuest I spoke to a man who had been physically attacked by "virotes," or magical darts. These psychic attacks cause the victim pain and can be life-threatening. The person under attack is usually not able to relieve the situation by themselves. The man told me he suddenly experienced severe pain in his chest and his good health began to deteriorate very quickly. During a healing ceremony, don Romulo withdrew several virotes from his chest, immediately relieving the man's pain. The man said he actually felt the virotes being pulled from his chest by don Romulo sucking them out of his body.

Howard Lawler says he chose don Romulo and Hermana Mari for SpiritQuest because of their impeccable integrity, though the majority of people practicing shamanism will work both sides: curanderismo and brujeria. According to Lawler's experience, it's hard to find pure curanderos who are not tempted to work on the dark side for a price.

The belief in life-threatening psychic attacks seems superstitious and naïve to us; however, in Peruvian life, virotes are a reality and are seriously addressed in the culture. In medieval times the same beliefs were held. Illnesses – whether physical or demonic – were treated with prayer and exorcism. Demon possession and demonic injury have existed in all cultures since antiquity. In Western society we have abandoned such concepts as ridiculous. Every malady – psychological, physical, and emotional – is given a clinical diagnosis and a prescription drug remedy.

**Conclusion**

I came away from SpiritQuest with the firm belief that religious writers, scientists, and philosophers studying consciousness need to explore revelatory states themselves before passing judgment on their authenticity. Only then can they fully understand the very similar dynamics of the mystical and ayahuascan experiences. Not to do so is akin to an acclaimed, world-renowned chef having never tasted food. What kind of faith would you have in his culinary skill?


**VICTORIA ALEXANDER** lives in Las Vegas with her husband Dr. John B. Alexander and is a contributor to *Films In Review*'s online magazine. She is a founding member of The Las Vegas Film Critics Society; a complete list of her movie reviews can be found on the influential film site Rottentomatoes.com. Victoria also writes a weekly column, The Devil's Hammer, for LasVegasRoundTheClock.

com and FromTheBalcony.com. Victoria's survey of 1000 theologians on the impact of UFOs on religion, "The Alexander UFO Religious Crisis Survey," is available at <www.nidsci.org>. She can be reached at kwanitaka@aol.com.

# BRAIN MECHANICS AND DISEMBODIED PHENOMENA
## BY DWIGHT G. SMITH AND GARY MANGIACOPRA

"It is with considerable difficulty that I remember the original era of my being: all the events of that period appeared confused and indistinct. A strange multiplicity of sensations seized me, and I saw, felt, heard, and smelt at the same time; and it was, indeed, a long time before I learned to distinguish between the operations of my various senses."
– Mary Shelly, *Frankenstein*

A wide range of human experience including near death experiences (NDE), out of body experiences (OBE), phantom limb feelings, schizophrenia, certain kinds of dreams and even the psyche itself and the contentious concept of consciousness may qualify as disembodied phenomena. All disembodied experiences are, by definition, out of the body experiences.

Concept and concern regarding these experiences is centuries old. Reports and recants were quite common during the Middle Ages and achieved a renewed popularity for a period during the Victorian Era of the mid-to-late 19th century when everyone, it seemed, wanted to compare and explore their disembodied experiences.

Even today these events achieve wide recognition and publicity as well. A recent Gallup poll found that over eight million Americans reported some kind of paranormal experience at least once during their lifetime and we can be sure that the actual percentage is probably much higher as many people are reluctant to report experiences that fall into the paranormal category. In fact, prior to open brain surgery, such stories were considered marks if not signals that someone had some mental problem that could only be addressed by professional psychiatric help. Perhaps that is the reason that they never really gained currency except as tabloid tales and fodder for New Age websites until the last few decades.

Today, disembodied phenomena are deemed sufficiently important that a number of medical, psychological, and neurological studies have been conducted to better explore and register the scientific roots, if any, of such phenomena. Thanks to developments in neuroscience, coupled with cutting edge technologies such as the latest brain scan devices, we are finally beginning to unravel the physical and physiological mechanisms that may stimulate certain types of disembodied experiences. At least some of these seem to center on the brain's way of recognizing itself and the body within which it lies.

## Concept of Self

One thing is for sure and that is the human mind has the ability to recognize and contemplate itself, which is almost certainly unique within the animal kingdom. The concept and uniqueness of own body imagery is centered firmly in the workings of the brain. Early on in our neurological development we become aware of ourselves as distinctive entities – that is, we repeat the progressive self-evolution of sense and sensation so cleverly portrayed by Mary Shelly's Frankenstein. This sense of self-image allows us to separate ourselves first from our parents and then from others.

The genesis of this self imagery must lie in the maturation of neural networks in the brain. Just as all of the trillions of cells in our body have chemical markers stamped "made in me," our mind develops a sense of proprietary distinctiveness as well, a sort of "I am myself and no one else." Again, as in Frankenstein's monster, it takes some time for this to happen. No doubt the phenomenon of self-imagery begins to develop almost immediately, probably even before birth, but progresses slowly through our infancy. Possibly as early as our third or fourth year of life our brain cements an awareness of how the body parts structurally fit together architecturally and is able to subconsciously achieve a visual spatial perspective or self-imagery.

Part of this self imagery concerns our distinctiveness and the other focuses on our body. Thus, we never have to look around for our arms or legs or other body parts because we "know" where they are. But what does this statement actually mean? A neuroscientist will explain that this is partly the result of special sensors called proprioceptors that are fitted in every muscle, bone, and fiber of our body. These sensors send a constant stream of information to our brain, which enables it to keep track of our position and orientation, at least with respect to our body. Traditionally, this information ends up in the sensory cortex of the brain, a broad region of that highly convoluted material near the surface of the brain that receives a constant information stream from all of our sensors such as pain, temperature, touch, and, of course, position of body parts and location of the body in time and space.

Awareness of bodily self and distinctiveness must lead to that other uniquely human phenomenon called consciousness – or did the act of being conscious lead to self awareness? Consciousness is another one of those scientific topics that awaits further research for absolute clarification, for consciousness contains a subjective component that, so far, transcends science experiments.

Part of the problem lies in the fact that there are different levels of consciousness. For example, asleep we are unconscious or nearly so, but under general anesthesia we are completely unconsciousness, if that is defined as being unaware of ourselves and our surroundings. In recognition of this lack of information, a recent issue of *Discover* magazine identified our lack of information about exactly what consciousness is as one of the ten unsolved mysteries of the brain in an article of the same name. The article, penned by David Eagleman, concluded that the state of consciousness can reside in a series of physical, chemical, molecular, or cellular levels and represent a circuitry of interrelated and interconnected events. Eagleman also pointed out that scientists are now working to identify brain locations that are active during the consciousness state.

This theme was repeated in an even more recent issue of the popular scientific journal called *Scientific American,* which featured a debate between two prominent neuroscientists regarding how neurons make us aware of ourselves, i.e., the concept of consciousness. We are concerned about what it is to be conscious because it is consciousness with all of its distinctiveness that allows us to recognize disembodied phenomena to begin with.

## Concept of Soul

The fact that we are, at least in our waking moments, conscious of ourselves, our distinctiveness, and our surroundings leads, in turn, to a more controversial and contentious topic and that is the existence of an individual soul. Because it is more often closely tied to religion, the concept and topic of a soul emanating within every human body and presumably every human mind draws biting sarcasm and criticism from a host of atheists but approval from others who believe that the soul is related to consciousness, which in turn is rooted in our self-perceived distinctiveness.

Regardless of soul and psyche, we must have some level of consciousness in order to be aware of out of body experiences so it must be that all of these events are interrelated brain functions.

## A Plethora of Disembodied Phenomena

The distinctiveness of self-recognition coupled with the mystifying nature of out of body experiences is illustrated by the variety of disembodied phenomena, a sampling of which is illustrated in the following tales:

• Item: A 66-year-old heart patient is undergoing a difficult valve replacement operation. Two hours into the operation her heart suddenly stops and shortly thereafter a flat EEG reading indicates that she is brain dead and has certifiably deceased. She calmly watches all this activity from an elevated perspective, just above the operating table as doctors frantically gather around to try and revive her. Their frantic efforts are successful and the patient tells yet another story of an Out of Body Experience (OBE).

• Item: Scientists report induction of an illusionary shadow person in a recent issue of *Nature* magazine. A 22-year-old female patient undergoing preliminary evaluation for surgical treatment of epilepsy reported the presence of a shadowy person whenever a segment of her left temporal-parietal junction (TPJ) was stimulated. The shadowy person did not speak to her and she was unable to feel it, but it closely shadowed and mimicked her movements. The shadow person responded to her every movement with a similar movement, even in one case merging "his" shadow into her body. She found the merging experience unpleasant and deeply disturbing.

• Item: Jessica lost her right arm in the course of a childhood accident many years ago. Now aged 42 and a mother of three, Jessica still has pains and aches from the missing limb. Sometimes these are so real and intense that she actually looks for the limb, momentarily forgetting that it was amputated long ago.

• Item: Well into the midst of a party night onboard a pleasure yacht a 42-year-old male falls overboard. After a number of minutes he is fished from the water. The man is unconsciousness and not breathing. The yacht reaches shore and an ambulance arrives. Emergency medical personnel are unable to find a pulse and the patient is pronounced dead at the scene and taken to the morgue. Following revival he relates a marvelous episode. He somehow knew that he had died but was unafraid. Instead, he found himself bathed in white light swiftly moving through a long corridor towards a distant destination. He didn't really walk along the corridor but rather "flowed" towards his destination. Long deceased relatives appeared on either side to welcome him and offer words of comfort and encouragement as he moved. Shortly later he is miraculously revived to enter the ranks of people that have undergone a Near Death Experience (NDE).

• Item: Ben is a quiet and serious child. He mixes well and plays often with other children in his age category and on the surface seems as normal as any nine-year-old can possibly be. But out of sight of others Ben is given to occasional bouts of introspection. Ben is, you see, desperately trying to separate fact from fiction, to sort out which is reality and which is made up. Therein lies the crux as most children can readily distinguish the real from the made-up, even during playtime and none would ever confuse a monopoly dollar with a real dollar bill, for example. Ben's source of concern is his dreams. He has recurrent dreams of another lifetime in another era. He even knows his real (or imagined) name, which was James Earl. Awake, he is a third grader, but asleep, he is always James Earl. Dream details are vivid and starkly realistic, so much so that Ben has come to believe that he actually was James Earl in a past life.

• Item: An individual identified only as a patient reported an occasional dream-like interlude during which she is equipped with three legs, all of which moved in unison. She further noted that the legs moved of their own accord as she watched them in spectator fashion.

• Item: A few years ago I reached that age in life where a colonoscopy was deemed necessary. I consented and duly arrived, in early morn, at the appointed time and appointed place. The colonoscopy apparently went extremely well. The last thing that I remember was telling the doctor: "I don't feel a bit sleepy." I awoke to hear the nurse telling me that I could get dressed now. But, I was already in the middle of getting dressed. The event remains vivid in my mind because I clearly remember becoming conscious (regaining consciousness) at that moment but I was already half dressed.

## Categorizing Disembodied Phenomena: A First Approach

*Out of Body Experiences (OBE):* Cognitive neurologist Olaf Blanke defines an OBE as an event that occurs when a person who is awake sees his or her body from a point or perspective outside of the body. The "awake" component of this definition does not follow every OBE reported, as in many cases the patients claim to be asleep or unconscious. Whatever the case, the OBE must inevitably be a most curious sensation for the individual undergoing them. Of these, probably the most familiar, or at least the most commonly reported OBE, involves looking down on the person's body from a height, often directly above the body. The experience includes watching other people looking at the immobile body along with everyone else, although sometimes the person experiencing the OBE is alone. Elevation is a variable as well; in some cases the person is viewing the body from a great height, in others they are at or near ceiling height.

*Autoscopy (AS):* Similar to OBE but in this context the individual views his or her body in extrapersonal space. This differs from an OBE in that the person undergoing an AS sees a projection of the body as if it were in front of, to the side, or behind the virtual body.

*Shadow Person Experiences:* This phenomenon is probably more closely allied to the concept of autoscopy. In this disembodied phenomenon the individual experient relates the presence of a nearby shadow person who is close to or sometimes touching the patient, typically from either immediately behind or directly in front of the virtual body. In some cases the shadow merges seamlessly, harmlessly, and painlessly with the patient so the two become one. In other cases the shadow follows the patient, exactly or almost mimicking their own movements. Still, the patient views the shadowy person as a separate entity but the physician interprets this as an OBE. Perhaps this kind of OBE experience is the basis for schizophrenia or the phenomenon of ghosts?

*Near Death Experiences (NDE):* One of the more popular versions of disembodied phenomena is near death experiences. In fact, they may figure just as importantly and frequently as OBE events. Although accounts of NDE vary greatly in details such as time length, time of day, and similar variables, most relate that they leave the body and move, usually in spirit form rather than body form towards a bright white light. Early interpreters of NDE suggested that during the ultimate moment of death the brain relives the moment of birth, when the person was leaving the birth canal to enter the brightly lit world. Other interpretations are also presented, but not really relevant to our discourse.

NDE phenomena began long before the movie *Flatliners*, which starred a young Julia Roberts, but at least some of the NDE stories from that movie were eerily similar to those reported from experients that underwent disembodied phenomena. Indeed, it has been suggested that disembodied phenomena provided the initial thought or stimuli for the movie, although this has never been documented to everyone's satisfaction. At any rate, *Flatliners* combined elements that we would commonly record as a combination of dreaming, OBE, and NDE in the sense that the person is observing events and antics of himself or herself. Not incidentally, it was intriguing to note that in the movie at least, these experiences were deliberately induced by temporary oxygen deprivation, which would also be the case in the NDE in which oxygen levels are, of course, dangerously low.

*Dreams and Dreaming:* Attempting to categorize dreams as one form of disembodied phenomena may or may not be realistic. Since no one knows exactly what dreams are and how they function in our homeostatic physiology (although none can deny that there are many "dream experts" out there), this suggestion is always open to interpretation and challenge. Consider two categories of dreams: in one, the dreamer has the sensation of being observed by another in the midst of the dream; in another, the dreamer is visiting or revisiting familiar landscapes, which may or may not include familiar faces and events. Since the dreamer is not actually conscious, could the act of dreaming comprise a disembodied phenomenon?

*Phantom Limbs:* These are rather commonly reported in the medical literature and usually concern military personnel who have lost one or more limbs during combat operations. For months and sometimes years afterwards some of these individuals report "feelings" or sensations from their arms or legs, which have long since been amputated. Individuals born without one or more limbs also occasionally report the phenomenon of phantom limbs. The most common medical and/or physiological explanation is that the limb has been removed but the neurons responsible for receiving information from and stimulating the amputated limb remain in the brain and may occasionally be activated when interconnected neurons fire. The phantom limb phenomenon reported by persons born without a particular limb is more difficult to resolve as these individuals presumably never did develop a limb-to-mind neural network.

**Keeping the Mind's Eye on Self**

The Ancient Greeks, for example, spoke with reverence and awe of the mind's power of "wind swift thought." More than a thousand years later it fell to French philosopher Renee Descartes to categorize the "id" of human ideology, of human recognition of being alive in his famous idiom "I think, therefore I am." From Descartes onwards everyone appreciates the singular fact that each of us are individuals with an individual basis and an individual consciousness. If disembodied phenomena can be recognized and are recognizable then it follows that they must somehow relate to changes or departures from the normal workings of the mind, long thought to be immutable.

In order to identify the mechanisms behind disembodied phenomena we must identify the workings of the mind with respect to how the mind processes self imaging information. One of the many basic mysteries of neurophysiology is where certain brain centers are located. That is, what parts of the brain code for, analyze, and direct different kinds of information. We know, for example, that the thalamus is for pain reception, the rhinocephalon for odor reception and the hippocampus is that part of the brain that stores temporary memory and also plays a role in transforming temporary memory into permanent memory. More difficult is determining brain sites or combination of sites that relate to our emotive senses such as personality, consciousness (again) and psyche. Furthermore, if only brain functions such as neuronal firings serve to maintain our visual self imagery along with all that is implicated in self attribution then it becomes reasonable to suggest that physical or chemical malfunctions of brain areas may be directly responsible for producing sensations of disembodied phenomena. For this, our question should be; can OBE and other disembodied experiences be explained only by brain malfunctions or do they represent an entirely unique paranormal phenomenon? To address this further we must examine and evaluate specific brain regions that have been most frequently identified with such experiences.

**Recent Experimental Studies**

*Self Imagery and Consciousness (again):* In order for us to understand how this part of the brain visualizes itself in space and time we also have to revisit concepts of brain derived consciousness. After all, we have to be conscious at some level in order to know that we are experiencing an OBE or any other type of disembodied phenomenon. Despite an intensive search that continues in neuroscience laboratories the world over, we do not know precisely which part of the brain is responsible for consciousness or psyche, but there are signs that we are closing in on this most intriguing subject. Dr. Stephen Laureys, for example, has compared studies of vegetative patients to conscious patients to detect differences in brain region activity and found some interesting results. For example, his group discovered that particular areas of the brain appear to be associated with that very complex state of being called consciousness. Using positron-emission topography (PET) they were able to identify brain regions that "appear to be particularly important for the emergence of awareness." They were able to detect a significant lack of metabolic activity in certain cortical areas of the frontal and parietal lobes of the brain that process sensory information. The group cautioned, however, that this thing called consciousness also most likely included deeper areas of the brain, including the thalamus, which is known to function in pain reception and also acts as a relay center for the transmission of incoming stimuli to higher brain levels.

Laureys also related the study of a 23-year-old woman who was in a vegetative state as a result of a brain injury suffered during a traffic accident. The study was conducted by a Cambridge University group and involved tracking brain activity using functional MRI scans of selected brain regions. Although vegetative and verbally unresponsive, the patient was asked to imagine walking through rooms in her house. Brain scans showed significant activity of the premotor, parietal, and parahippocampal cortices, which are all part of the spatial navigation network of the human brain. The key component of interest here is the role the parietal plays in spatial navigation plus the fact that a specific region of the brain does, in fact, play an important role in how the self or the body is viewed or realized in space, a scope typing body location, movement, and consciousness to the body.

*Inducing Out-of Body Experiences:* The August 24, 2007 issue of the very prestigious journal *Science* reported results of two very recently concluded scientific experiments aimed at elucidating the neurophysiology of these events.

In one experiment, cognitive neuroscientists Bigna Lenggenhager and Olaf Blanke of the Swiss Federal Institute of Technology induced what they describe as an OBE by having participants wear video-display goggles that recorded and displayed a computer enhanced three dimensional view of their own back. As the participants watched the video display, their video displayed backs were stroked with a highlighter pen. The participants felt that their virtual body back was, in fact, really their back.

In another study reported in the same issue of *Science*, Dr. Henrik Ehrsson of University College London and the Institute of Neurology in Stockholm, Sweden, reported inducing an OBE in normally healthy volunteers. The experimental protocol involved seating a participant in a chair equipped with head mounted displays that portrayed different images of the person's back simultaneously to the right and left eye. That way the person ended up viewing their own back just as they would if they were sitting behind another person. Then came the multi-sensory information that triggered the out of body illusion. As the experimenter stood outside of the subject's point of view, he used two plastic rods to simultaneously touch the subject's real and virtual chest. Subjects afterwards completed a questionnaire aimed at rating the effectiveness of the illusionary experiences. Based on survey results, Ehrsson concluded that participants were undergoing an induced out-of-body experience. Ehrsson conducted one additional experiment in which he attached electrodes to his subjects' fingers to measure electrical current or skin conductance. While the participant watched himself or herself a hammer struck an unseen region of their virtual body positioned just outside the view of the camera. Ehrsson found that the participants reacted with fear, as if the subject's sense of "self" had left his physical body and shifted to the virtual one. On the basis of these findings, Ehrsson again concluded that he had artificially induced an OBE through his camera experiments.

But Ehrsson's results drew immediate criticism. No one doubts or denies that the experiments were conducted correctly and conformed to strict scientific protocol. Rather, the contention lies in connecting these versions of OBE with those reported by others as naturally occurring phenomena (or unnaturally occurring phenomena). Ehrsson begins by defining an OBE as an experience in which an awake individual sees their body from a perspective or location from outside of the body, something which may or may not be true of all reported OBE phenomena. Certainly it does not apply to people undergoing a NDE or most of the other categories of disembodied phenomena previously described. A second and perhaps equally valid criticism is that the method of inducing OBE perceptions differ little, if at all, from what occurs when we enter a carnival or amusement park "funhouse" and are confronted with multiple images of ourselves in a room of mirrors.

*Studies Focusing on the TPJ:* An earlier series of studies by Dr. Olaf Blanke attempted to locate that part, or those parts, of the brain that are responsible for maintaining the perception the body's self image; that is, how does and where does the brain keep track of the borders of physical body? These studies were conducted in a number of ways but mostly centered on patients who related one or more out of body experiments. All of Blanke's patients had either lesions or epilepsy problems associated with the temporal-parietal junction (TPJ) located in the brain's left hemisphere. It further appears that a specific part of the TPJ called the angular gyrus is most closely associated with body self imaging. The angular gyrus is located just underneath the junction of the temporal and parietal bone. Also called the gyrus angularis, it is that part of the parietal lobe just behind the supramarginal gyrus and immediately below the temporal lobe.

Studies have identified certain functions with this part of the brain, specifically that it is responsible, at least in part, for processes involved in language. This area is also called Brodmann area 39 of the brain. We do know that this whole segment is involved in language understanding and seems to be the area that translates writing into meaning. That is, as we read this page it is the angular gyrus that makes the chemical signals intelligible by somehow translating those chemical signals into an internal dialogue that mimics speech, at least for our brain. It is also the area of the brain that relates words and language concepts to other senses. For example, this is the part of the brain that permits us to "see" an orange and remember its color and smell.

The angular gyrus's role in establishing the position and self imagery of the body may be due to its placement at the intersection or crossroads of a number of sensory inputs. It is significant that the angular gyrus lies directly at the junction of those areas of the brain that are responsible for processing modalities of touch, hearing, and vision, all of which provide cues that may help the body keep track of itself on a moment-to-moment basis. Basically, this part of the brain is able to acquire and integrate information from tactile, proprioceptors, visual and vestibular input to maintain constant visual spatial perspective regarding the body and its parts. Therefore, any chemical or physical malfunction of this part of the brain, including induced stimuli, may result in changes in our own body imagery.

## The Crypto Connection

Almost all disembodied experiences, but especially OBEs, are life-changing phenomena for experients. Most report a mystic or religious experience that generally lasts a lifetime. This is especially evident in those individuals who have had a NDE---almost uniformly, they report a renewed intensity of religious feelings, peace, wellness, and seem to have an entirely different attitude towards the finality of death. Other forms of out of body experiences are more mystical and perhaps provide a link to concepts of psyche and soul.

A malfunctioning of certain areas of the brain, which produces a neurological disorder, may produce sensations that are associated with paranoia, persecution, alien presence, alien abduction, alien control, and others. Is it far too speculative to suggest that alien abduction may result from unusual chemical or physical manifestations originating from a portion of the brain? Again, consider the 22-year-old female who was convinced that she was being followed by a shadow person, which in reality represented her brain's perceived placement of her body. Even the slight bodily displacement she experienced resulted in an illusion that seemed perfectly real. Who can possibly doubt that the brain is really responsible for keeping track of body orientation? If we accept this as a biological fact tantamount to a biological law, then it certainly follows that any malfunction, however slight, of this all-important ability of the brain can produce slight and sometimes serious alterations of our perceptions of ourselves with respect to body and disembodied experiences?

Whatever the case, a satisfactory medical and neurological explanation for at least some categories of out of body experiences may provide the physiological link for those who report sensations of being watched or alien abduction and for schizophrenia. Considerations of crypto factors such as ghosts, aliens, being watched, shadow persons, for example, may now be linked to chemical malfunctions of the TPJ, which may be temporary or permanent. The conclusion that inherent mysticism associated with the varieties of out of body experiences may be completely linked to temporary disassociations in a specific part of the brain is not an especially satisfactory conclusion for cryptobiologists who will want to follow emerging developments in this field closely.

Finally, what of the relationship – if any – between disembodied phenomena and consciousness? We can begin by asking just what being conscious is and how it operates within the brain or perhaps how the brain operates to produce consciousness. Is being conscious just the fortuitous byproduct generated by gigantic increases in neurological activity while we are awake, for example, as both Susan Greenfield and Christof Koch seem to suggest in their article in *Scientific American*? If so, do the various reports of disembodied phenomena relate directly or indirectly to degrees of being conscious?

At the very least, we now have real science finally addressing basic questions of paranormal phenomena.

## References

Note, dozens of interesting and unusual books, articles, papers, and web sites are listed in the 12 page online *Wikipeida* article entitled "Near Death Experiences." Readers intrigued by the science behind the various disembodied phenomena should first read the series of papers by Olaf Blanke, who has spent decades as neuroscientist at the University Hospital of Geneva. Most of his papers may also be accessed online at <brain.oxfordjournals.org/cgi/content/full/127/2/243> for a detailed summary of his work to which is appended an extensive reference section, most of which also is available for online access.

Arzy, Shahar, Margitta Seeck, Stephanie Ortigue, Laurent Spinelli, and Olaf Blanke. 2006. "Induction of an illusory shadow person. Stimulation of a site on the brain's left hemisphere prompts the creepy feeling that someone is close by." *Nature* 43: 287.

Blackmore, S. 1992. *Beyond the body. An investigation of out of body experiences.* London: Heinemann Publishing Company.

Blanke, Olaf, S. Ortigui, T. Landis, M. Seeck. 2002. "Inducing illusory own body perceptions." *Nature* 419: 29-270.

Blanke, Olaf, Theodor Landis, Laurent Spinelli, and Margitta Seeck. 2004. "Out-of-body experience and autoscopy of neurological origin." *Brain* 127: 243-258.

Blanke, Olaf, Christine Mohr, Christopher Michel, Alvaro Pascual-Leone, Peter Brugger, Margitta Seeck, Theodor Landis and Gregor Thut. 2005. "Linking out-of-body experience and self processing to mental own-body imagery at the temporolparietal junction." *Journal of*

*Neuroscience* 25: 550-557.

Bonda, E., M. Petrides, S. Frey, and M. Evans. 1995. "Neuro correlates of mental transformations of the body-in-space." *Proceedings National Academy of Sciences* 92: 11180-11184.

Bosveld, Jane. 2007. "Soul Search: Can science ever decipher the secrets of the human soul?" *Discover*, "Special Issue: Science, Technology and the Future." June 2007 issue: 47-50.

Crick, F., and C. Koch. 2003. "A framework for consciousness." *Nature Neuroscience* 6: 119-126.

Downing, P. E., Y. Jiang, M. Shuman, N. Kanwisher. 2001. "A cortical area selective for visual processing of the human body." *Science* 293: 2470-2473.

Eagleman, David. 2007. "10 unsolved mysteries of the brain." *Discover* August 2007 issue, pages 54-59, 75.

Ehrsson, H. H. 2007. "The experimental induction of Out-of-Body Experiences." *Science* 317: 1048.

Lenggenhager, B., T. Taji, T. Metzinger and Olafe Blanke. "Video Ergo Sum: Manipulating body self-consciousness." *Science* 317: 1096. With supporting materials online.

Greenfield, Susan. 2003. *The private life of the brain*. John Wiley and Sons.

Greenfield, Susan. 2005. "A neuroscientific approach to consciousness." *Progress in Brain Research* 150: 11-23.

Irwin, H. J. 1985. *Flight of mind; a psychological study of the out-of-body experience*. Lanham: Scarecrow Press.

Koch, Christof, and Susan Greenfield. 2007. "How does consciousness happen?" *Scientific American* 297: 76-83.

Kolb, Bryan, and Ian Q. Whishaw. 2006. *An introduction to brain and behavior*. Second Edition. Worth Publishing. New York, New York.

Laureys, Stephen. 2005. "Science and Society, Unconsciousness and the brain." *Nature Reviews in Neuroscience* 6 (11): 899-909.

Laureys, Stephen. 2007. "Eyes open, brain shut." *Scientific American* 84-89. May 2007.

Neisser, U. 1988. "Five kinds of self knowledge." *Philos. Psychology* 1: 35-59.

Vogelcy, K., G. R. Fink. 2003. "Neurocorrelates of the first person perspective." *Trends Cognitive Science* 7: 38-42.

Zacks, M., J. M. Ollinger, M. A. Sheridan, B. Tversky. 2002. "A panametric study of mental spatial transformations of bodies." *Neuroimage* 16: 857-872.

**DWIGHT SMITH** teaches biology at Southern Connecticut State University in New Haven, Connecticut.

**GARY MANGIACOPRA** is a researcher living in Milford, Connecticut.

# IN TOUCH WITH OTHER WORLDS
## By Mark Macy

I have been an atheist or agnostic as far back as I can remember. Notions of God and afterlife seemed like wishful thinking to me. Then in 1988 I was diagnosed with colon cancer, and with death staring me in the face, suddenly I had to know what *really* happens to us after we die. I couldn't take it on faith—not that there's anything wrong with faith—but I've always needed proof or good, solid evidence to convince me of something beyond my understanding. And afterlife was way beyond my understanding.

Then in 1991 I attended a New Sciences conference in Fort Collins, Colorado, and ran into an old fellow named George Meek who took a technical approach to researching the afterlife. He was regarded as the father of ITC, or Instrumental Trans-Communication,

*George Meek photographs himself having an out-of-body experience.*

which is the use of technology to get in touch directly with the other side. George told me some mind-boggling things at the conference.

One day George went down to his basement lab with a 35-mm camera and tripod and set up the camera to take a long series of pictures automatically under special lighting. He then sat in a chair, meditated, and had an out-of-body experience that he captured on film.

George also told me that he and another fellow named Bill O'Neil had developed a device they called a "Spiricom," which is short for "spirit communication." From 1979 to 1981, O'Neil would stand in front of the Spiricom device and talk to someone on the other side of the veil the way that you or I might stand in front of a speakerphone and talk to someone on the other side of town. These were the first known dialogs between "Heaven" and Earth using special equipment, since "the voice of God" spoke to Moses and his brother Aaron through the legendary Ark of the Covenant. George Meek announced the Spiricom breakthrough to the world at the National Press Club in Washington DC, fittingly, on Easter morning 1982.

He then told me that shortly after his wife Jeannette died in 1991, she sent George a picture and letter through a computer in Europe

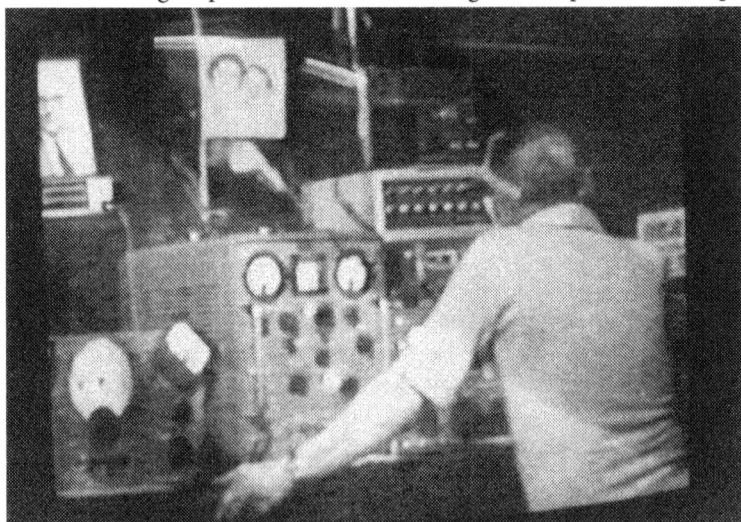

*Bill O'Neil and Spiricom*

while George was at home in North Carolina. The letter related three very personal incidents from their life together –incidents that only the two of them could possibly know about. One had to do with a lost key to a tenant's house; another, a box of books lost in shipment; and the third, a yard light installed outside their house. These were incidents of no importance to anyone, not even to George, but they proved conclusively that the mind, memory, and personality of his wife Jeannette lived on after the death of her physical body. The picture showed Jeannette in the paradise world she was living in now. Both items were planted in the computer of Maggy and Jules Harsch-Fischbach of Luxembourg, who were friends and colleagues of George Meek.

If George Meek's claims were true, I thought, then this was exactly the kind of good evidence I would need to be convinced of an afterlife. I was so fascinated by his work that George invited me to his home and research lab in Franklin, North Carolina. He would soon introduce me to fellow researchers in Europe and South America, and within a year I would be swept away by findings and experiences that would change my life forever.

• • •

Most of the breakthroughs in technical communication beyond the Earth have taken place across the Atlantic, in Europe. It started in the 1950s, when audiotaping became popular around the world. People would tape music, conversations, or nature sounds, and sometimes when playing it back they'd hear short, faint voices on the tape – voices that by all rational thought should not be there. The voices could rarely be heard during taping – only on playback. Swedish filmmaker Friedrich Juergenson and Latvian psychologist Konstantin Raudive become pioneers in the electronic voice phenomenon, or EVP. They recorded and catalogued tens of thousands of these tiny voices and challenged science to come up with an explanation.

In the 1960s an Italian researcher named Marcello Bacci began experimenting with an AM radio. He received the first known direct voice through that radio in 1970. A direct voice, unlike an EVP voice, can be heard as it's created. It often bursts through, loud and

```
eneber…
nbegrenzt,aber a_
nverstaendnisundverze₁.
chreibendaseinenueberkommtwe…
ichtzuangesichtredenkann/vorallemueber…
hierzueeuchdurchstellenberatenwirunsmitdemratderhoe…
choderandereunserergruppebeiwohnendarf/diesgeschiehtiineinemrunde
nraumdessenwaendenachallenseitenhindurchsichtigsind/waehrendderge
spraechedrehtderraumsichumsichselbstundmansiehtaussenlichter,form
enundfarbenvorbeiziehendievonatemberaubenderschoenheitsind/leises
pharenmusikerfuelltdenhintergrund/thomasisteinteilderwesenheitset
h3undinihmenthalten/umeseuchzubeschreibenkoennteichsagendasserand
iesnversammlungenteilnimmtindemeraufeinembildschirmewrscheint,wae
hrenddereigentlicheseth3alsmanninmittlerenjahrenselbstanwesendist
/dietechnikerberatenundleitenunsabersiezensurierenunsnicht/dielet
zteentscheidunguebergesandtesmaterialliegtbeiunsselbstunwirversuc
hennurdaszueuchdurchzustellen,wasvonallenhiergutgeheissenwird/sta
endigko…mennevemitgliederbeiunsanabernichtallenamenwuerdeneuchetw
assagen…oh…tenwirinddenletztentagenfolgendeneuzugaenge:guystaff
ausucc…lgien/franzschliffenbacherausgrafingindeutschland/bhe
gien…amstelveeninholland/luigisaltarinausmilanoinitalien/ala
intoc…entingeninluxemburg/eienliebefreundinvonmir,jeannetteme
ekmoe…taandieserstelleeinigeworteaninhrenaufeuereseiteweilendenga
ttenrichten/ichubergebeihrdenzeilensender/
DEARGW/I'DLIKETOCOOKUPAFEWGOODNAMESFORYOUBELIEVINGICOULDHAVEWINGS
!IAMSUREYOURECALLIHAVEOFTENTOLDYOUTHATTHEREARELOTSOFTHINGSYOUCOME
INHANDYFOR---
NOTONLYTODO(SUCHASTAKECAPSOFPILLBOTTLES)BUTALSOTOTELLSOMEBODYELSE
JUSTWHATTODO(EXPERTADVICE)/WELL,ITSEEMSASIFTHEREARESTILLPEOPLEWHO
DONOTBELIEVINTHECONTACTSYOURFRIENDSOFCETLAREHAVING/HERESOMEDETAIL
SWHICHEXCEPTYOUANDMOLLY(GIVEHERMYWARMESTGREETINGS,IMISSHER)NOBODY
CANKNOW/:IN1987,ENDOFAPRIL,TENANTDEBBIECALLEDTOSAYHERREFRIGERATOR
WASOFF/ITMUSTHAVEBEENONATHURSDAYMORNINGANDNOCONNECTIONWITHTHESTOR
MWEHADBEFORE/ATTHECLOSEOFHERWORKDAYSHECALLEDAGAINTOSAYSHEWASHAVIN
GM,ORETROUBLE/THISTIMESHEHADLEFTHERPURSEONTHESEATOFTHECAROFTHELAD
YWITHWHOMSHEHADBEENRIDING/THISLADYWASQUITEFARFROMFRANKLINSODEBBIE
ASKEDTOBORROWOURKEYTOHERPLACE/ANOTHERSTORY:ONAPRIL29THANNVALENTIN
WROTEALETTERTHATSHEHADNOTRECEIVEDTHEMAGICBOOKLETSTHEYHADORDERD,BU
THARLEQUINNOVELS/THIRDSTORY:JOHNLATHROP(IDON'TTHINKMAGGIEANDJULES
EVERHEARDTHISNAME)SHUTOFFTHEELECTRICITYATTHECHOUSETOPUTINTHENEWLI
GHT/HEWASN'TDOWNTHEREVERYLONGBUTCHARGED$20SERVICEADDITIONTO$40FOR
THEBULBITSELFPLUSTAX(THESCOUNDREL)/SOTRYTOEXPLAINTHIS,HONEY/MYNEV
ERENDINGLOVETOYOU/IMISSYOUSOMUCHBUTIKNOWWWEWILLBETOGETHER/IHAVEBI
GWORKTODOHERE/RESULTOFTHATIDIOTWAR/LOVEFOREVER/JtoM/
pleasemaggy/forwardthistogeorge/hecanbeofgreathelptoyouall/sendmy
bestwishestoloreealso/thankyou/jeannetteduncanmeek/kontaktende/..
```

*George Meek received this picture and letter from his wife Jeannette after her death.*

clear, "into thin air." For several decades, then, guests would gather in Marcello Bacci's basement and listen to disembodied voices talk through his radio. Many of his guests believed they were listening to their departed loved ones. Examples of the messages that came through Bacci's radio include: *"You know this is not easy for us,"* and, *"At the center of eternity where there is only good, everything is smooth vibration."* That center is what time-proven religions have come to call God, Allah, Yahweh, or Brahman.

In 1974 a German electroacoustical technician named Hans-Otto Koenig heard about the electronic voice phenomenon and set out to prove that the voices came from experimenters' unconscious minds, not from spirits, as he didn't believe in the existence of spirits. But when Koenig heard his late mother's singing voice suddenly break through his radio sounds, addressing him and his father by name, Koenig was forced to rethink his assumption.

Following his inner guidance, Koenig built a radio system consisting of 10 quartz crystals connected to LCDs and phototransistors, all feeding into a stochastic generator, or random noise generator, that produced FM radio waves, which in turn were converted to an audio signal. A spirit group calling themselves "C e n t r a l e" quickly formed around his efforts and became proficient at speaking clearly through the audio sounds of Hans-Otto

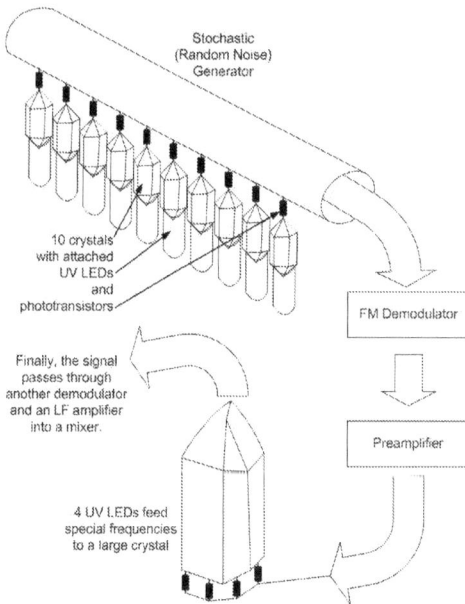

Stochastic (Random Noise) Generator

10 crystals with attached UV LEDs and phototransistors

FM Demodulator

Finally, the signal passes through another demodulator and an LF amplifier into a mixer.

Preamplifier

4 UV LEDs feed special frequencies to a large crystal

*Hans-Otto Koenig's radio device*

Koenig's crystalline radio device. On one occasion they referred to a "contact field," a resonant pool of attitudes and intentions of everyone on both sides of the veil who were involved in a communication project, and they said that the contact field was very important for these communications. Another time they warned: *"Assuming that Jesus Christ died for your sins is seen by some of us on this side as an attempt to shirk your responsibilities."*

It was becoming evident that of the most prolific ITC researchers had innate mediumistic skills, which seemed to play a key role in opening the communication bridge to the spirit worlds. They exuded some kind of life energy that affected the world(s) around them in profound ways that were for the most part indiscernible to us on Earth, but those on the other side of the veil could actually see the effects of those researchers' thoughts and intentions. They were quietly creating forms and structures and building communication bridges with their minds and their focused will.

Klaus Schreiber of Germany was a good example of a prolific researcher possessing strong psychic skills. Schreiber learned about the spoon-bending phenomenon in the 1970s (some people could relax their mind, focus their intention, and gently stroke a spoon until it began to bend, with little or no pressure from the hand), and he quickly discovered that not only silverware, but horseshoes would become soft and pliable to his touch. Many of Schreiber's family members had died, and as he reflected sadly on the loss of his loved ones, sometimes he'd hear their voices speaking quietly in his mind, or in ambient sounds. In 1982 he began

*EVP-ITC pioneers Friedrich Juergenson, Konstantin Raudive, Marcello Bacci, Hans-Otto Koenig, and Klaus Schreiber.*

to experiment with these sounds, especially radio sounds, and he was able to capture the voices of his departed loved ones on audiotape. Before long he began to see their faces on his TV set.

Electronic technician Martin Wenzel helped Schreiber set up a video camera to output to TV, so that whatever they filmed would be seen on the TV screen. They mounted the camera on a tripod and aimed it directly at the TV to create a feedback loop, and video ITC took a giant leap forward. A cloud of visual noise would broil and build on the screen, and out of that cloud would emerge faces – faces of Klaus Schreiber's deceased daughter Karin, his brother Robert, and other loved ones, as well as faces of strangers and famous people such as Austrian actress Romy Schneider and scientist Albert Einstein.

*Schreiber's TV images of Romy Schneider and his daughter Karin.*

It was becoming clear that audio and visual feedback (an unstable condition as when a microphone is moved in front of a speaker) could facilitate ITC contacts. Schreiber's voice contacts included messages saying: *"I come to you, Klaus, in a picture,"* and *"Hello, Klaus, I'm here again. It's simply beautiful here, Klaus; we don't live in the cemetery."* They were reminding Schreiber (and humanity in general) that the living human spirit leaves the body and the Earth upon death and moves to a beautiful paradise existence. Life continues; it doesn't end in a cemetery.

Chats between Heaven and Earth were becoming like chats between friends; sometimes they were technical, sometimes philosophical, sometimes informative, sometimes mundane.

A Luxembourg schoolteacher named Maggy Harch-Fischbach began to experiment with microphone recordings in the summer of

1985, with the intention of carrying the work of Bacci, Koenig and Schreiber to a new level. "I wanted to open the doors to the other world a little wider," she says modestly. As Maggy's results improved, her husband Jules Harsch joined her experiments, and in the spring of 1986 they had their first breakthrough when a loud, clear voice exclaimed through the radio sounds, "Here it is summer, always summer!"

A door seemed to have opened up for them. As the months passed, their small flat became a place of miracles. The radio voices became long and clear. Maggy began to receive phone calls from a spirit group calling themselves "Timestream," which was named for the challenge the spirit group faced in adjusting to the flow of time in our world. Time in their world, they said, is nebulous. Images of people and places on the other side began to appear on the Harsch-Fischbach couple's TV screen and to show up as bit maps on the hard disk of their computer. The couple also began to find long text messages in their computer. They were told that the amazing breakthroughs were facilitated by ethereal beings – angels – who were giving the couple a small taste of the future possibilities of ITC.

On one occasion these highly advance beings told the couple: *"Fear of death is one of the most distressing concepts of human culture. It is based on the conscious belief that your bodily existence offers life and security, which it never wants to lose. Fear of death, therefore, is evidence of the mind having lost its roots. It shows a spiritual being who has far removed itself from its higher self. It is the result of an intellectual and scientific way of thinking that wants all thoughts reduced to a comprehensible aspect of material existence."*

On another occasion the ethereal beings spoke of three phases of ITC on Earth. In the first phase (1979-89), they said, ITC contacts were like mediumistic contacts – channeled through human minds – before coming through the equipment. The second phase (1985-95) showed that the contacts are not dependent on human psyches, as some messages and images began to come through equipment in a pure, unfiltered condition. And in the future, the ethereal beings said, *"the third phase of ITC will depend on researchers and experimenters scattered all over the world achieving and sustaining a spiritual unity. Only then can the equipment provide a stable link to our spheres without going through the human psyche.*"

Now all Heaven was starting to break loose as it became clear that teams of competent, good-natured, optimistic men- and women-in-spirit were coming together on the other side, forming spirit groups for the purpose of opening free-streaming communication bridges to our world.

• • •

And that's where I came into the ITC picture. After meeting George Meek in 1991, I flew to Europe to meet some European researchers, especially the Luxembourg couple, Maggy and Jules Harsch-Fischbach. It was a life-changing trip. I entered their lab on Marie Curie Boulevard in downtown Luxembourg and was welcomed by a 19th-Century chemist named Henri Sainte Claire de Ville, on behalf of the Timestream spirit group. Obviously, de Ville didn't show up "in person," but delivered a message to an old green-screen computer monitor running MS-DOS. The message said, in part, *"This is Henri Sainte Claire de Ville, member of the Scientific Group. We were unable to link Timestream and Centrale in joint efforts for a successful cross-contact last weekend. It's a vibrational problem that will require a minor adjustment to your device. We warmly greet Mark Macy and Hans Heckmann. Please tell George Meek that I am no longer with Project Lifeline, but work with Marie Curie, who is in charge of the Scientific Group."*

Earlier the couple had received TV and radio contacts from the late scientist, who showed his face and said, *"My name is Henri Sainte Claire de Ville. I left your world in 1881, and I am speaking to you in my name, and in the name of our group of Lifeline, the Scientists. Your purpose, as well as Lifeline's and Timestream's, is to set fire to minds. To set fire to minds in your world, and in that moment to try to master time."*

I began to work closely with the Harsch-Fischbach couple, exchanging faxes with them several times a week and publishing the results of their experiments in books, audiocassettes, and journals. As months passed it became evident that our efforts were being directed toward the third phase of ITC. It was time for researchers and experimenters scattered around the world to join together in spiritual unity. Our ethereal friends had told us that only then could stable ITC systems be sustained, allowing brilliant information to stream into our world from finer realms of spirit, without being filtered by individual human minds.

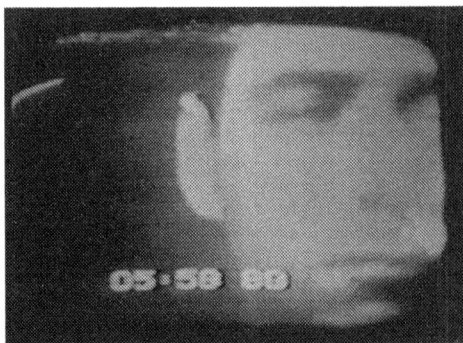

*Nineteenth Century chemist Henri Sainte Claire de Ville appearing on TV.*

I began to feel as if I'd been groomed without my conscious knowledge to help on this project. Before my colon cancer and spiritual search, I had spent 15 years devising a system approach to life – uncovering patterns common to human affairs, world affairs, and the affairs of the entire natural world, ranging from cells and molecules to plants and animals, to vast forests and oceans. I was trying to figure out what caused peace, order, and stability in life, and what caused conflict, chaos, and suffering – some simple principle that might allow people to get along with each other and with the planet.

Well, I came up with a principle – actually, a set of principles – that turned out to be rather basic and uncomplicated. For example, a popular concept in the peace community in the mid 1980s was "conflict resolution." I reasoned that people might have more success sustaining unity if they spent more effort not just resolving conflicts but *minimizing* conflicts by adopting what I called compatible standards and values. Wouldn't it be nice if everyone in the world had the same kind of plugs on their appliances; drove on the same side of the street; shared the same basic knowledge of wholesome nutrition; had the same knowledge of the vast universe around us and the infinitely complex universe inside us; understood the basic biological, emotional, and mental differences between boys and girls, men and women; and knew how to take those differences into account when communicating with each other? Wouldn't it be nice if there were recommended norms on just about everything—norms that would be adopted at the global level so that they could trickle down through governments and communities, into schools and families? Wouldn't that bring our world closer to a sustained peace and stability than ever before possible? And wouldn't that be possible today with the internet? Wouldn't such steps toward compatibility nip most conflict in the bud? I believed (and still do) that the answer to all of those questions would be a resounding, "Yes!"

So, armed with such theories of peace and unity, I worked with the Harsch-Fischbach couple in 1995 to establish the International Network for Instrumental Transcommunication (INIT). Thirteen researchers from eight countries met in Dartington, England, to sign a mission statement and forge a constitution. Our purpose was to take a moral, ethical approach to ITC and, in so doing, to sustain harmony among researchers in the coming years.

We then enjoyed five years of unprecedented miracles. Many of our members received phone calls from our invisible friends at Timestream. I had some breakthroughs in my radio experiments as well, and our spirit friends sent a series of mind-boggling images and messages to us through the computers of our Luxembourg members. For example, the ethereal beings told us what it's like from their perspective when they come to Earth to take us humans "home" at the end of our earthly lives. They also told us of a time long before recorded history when an Eden-like paradise did in fact exist, how it was destroyed, and how modern man fits into the resulting picture. I examine such ethereal messages in my recent book, *Spirit Faces*.

We were told that many forces had to come together on both sides of the veil to make the miracle of ITC possible, and one of the main factors on our side was resonance among INIT members, which we managed to sustain until around 2000. Then human foibles began to take over. Doubts, insecurities, fears, and envy led to false accusations of fraud, which escalated into counter-attacks and calls for the dismissal of various members, who eventually broke away and started a new association. The mistrust and general dissonance between (and within) the two groups ruined the contact field. The new association received no major contacts whatsoever, and the contacts of the now hobbling INIT group diminished steadily until they disappeared altogether. The age-old disclaimer, "We're only human," took on stunning new meaning as the miracle of the ages died before our eyes.

• • •

So for seven years ITC miracles have ceased, perhaps as part of an overall plan. We seem to be in a period of regrouping. After 15 years in the work, I'm convinced that ITC is mostly beyond our control and is choreographed by the minds of ethereal beings who say they have followed our world for tens of thousands of years. These ethereal beings, who seem omniscient from our perspective (but who assure us that they too have limitations), have given us a taste of the possibilities of ITC, but the bridges cannot or will not open wide until the stage is set.

Not only do we lack the needed understanding of the spirit worlds and the subtle energy technologies that would make other-worldly communications easier, but there are things out of joint in our world too. Again, a key consideration in other-worldly pursuits is resonance. As the communication bridges with the other side begin to open wide, we have to ask ourselves with whom we expect to communicate. The answer is simply that we will communicate with anyone in the spirit worlds who resonates with our attitudes. That's simply the way things operate in this complex multidimensional omniverse, as the spirit friends told us through ITC systems a decade ago, and as explained in the popular DVD, *The Secret*. We may *want* to communicate with Einstein or Gandhi or Jesus or Mohammed or Gautama or a cluster of ethereal beings, but a group of people with an open ITC channel *will* communicate with beings who resonate with their attitudes. If it's a group of people driven by love and harmony and good wishes for the entire planet, then yes, there is a chance they can get in touch with those fine and brilliant entities. On the other hand, if it's a group of people who are driven by egos who try to outdo each other or are driven by fears, animosities, resentment, or suspicion of other groups and cultures, then that group will get in touch with mischievous entities who will enjoy stirring up those troubled feelings even more. For every human emotion, there are many spirits on the other side who can and do resonate with it.

That, in a nutshell, is why ITC today is at a crossroads. It's not a lack of technology; experience has proven that the technologies present today can be accessed by a competent spirit group with the help of ethereal beings, although subtle energy technologies of the future should make it easier for them. It's not a desire of people to be in touch with the other side; most people today, overcoming the initial trepidation of the unknown, would probably love to get a phone call from dear, departed Auntie Rose or Abe Lincoln or Mahatma Gandhi or Albert Schweitzer or . . . .

It's not technology or desire; it's attitude. We have to learn how to come to terms with our humanness – to move our fears, doubts, and insecurities to the back burner, and to bring our love, trust, and sense of decency to the forefront. That's the key to a beautiful future of ITC – what the ethereals have called *"a fruitful, endurable relationship with the light, ethereal realms of existence."*

Meanwhile, researchers like myself work tirelessly to spread the word about ITC and spirituality, to provide good, solid evidence to help influence the more skeptical among us, especially scientists, and to do the inner work necessary to keep us in the right frame of mind so that we resonate with "the good guys" on the other side. I think it's just a matter of time before the bridges open wide and humanity enters a new Golden Era the likes of which have never been seen in this world before, thanks to ITC.

• • •

I've put most of my radio and telephone efforts on hold since the ITC bridge has been temporarily shut down for seven years, but I use a device called a "luminator" to gather good, solid evidence – virtual proof that the spirit worlds exist and they're not far off in space somewhere as we often tend to think; they're right here, all around us, separated from our world not by distance but by vibration, like radio waves all jumbled together in the same space but remaining distinct by their frequencies. I use a simple Polaroid camera to take pictures of people in the presence of the luminator, and very often

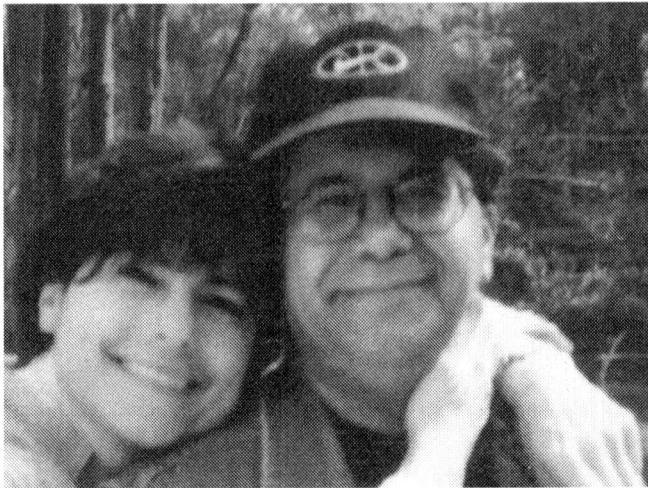

John Alberti died suddenly in 1994, and his wife Debbie attended my seminar at the Edgar Cayce Center a few months later. Of several

pictures I took of Debbie, most came out fairly clear, as in the picture just to the left (although notice her arm, which indicates spiritual presence). In one picture (lower left) a spirit face appeared at Debbie's throat. A closer look (below) revealed two separate spirit faces divided diagonally. Debbie says the lower left half-face is definitely her husband John, and I believe the other half face (upper right) belongs to Edgar Cayce (lifetime photo printed courtesy of the Edgar Cayce Foundation).

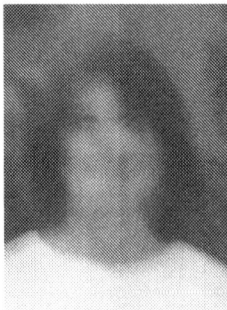

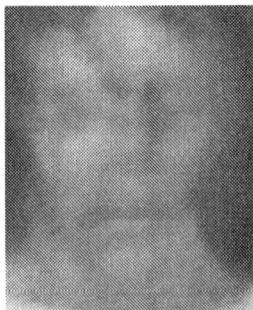

when the pictures develop a few minutes later, it's not just the human subject in the frame, but also a spirit guide or departed loved one, or a member of my spirit group, or simply an invisible stranger who happens to be present during the photo shoot. So the luminator lets me get very simple ITC contacts in a mixed crowd on a fairly reliable basis. Beyond that, I don't do much experimenting at the moment.

In the larger picture of ITC research, in which images and vivid descriptions of the other side can be planted on computer hard drives by invisible hands, and spirit friends can talk to us on the phone for upwards of fifteen minutes, the spirit faces I get in the presence of the luminator are not very dramatic. They show us how the human spirit looks when it's in dense realms near the physical world; they provide proof of an afterlife; they sometimes give some degree of solace to people who are grieving the death of a loved one; and they allow spirit to make its presence known in our world.

But beyond that, the luminator images don't offer any deep insights into life on the other side. Nor do they allow us to enjoy a meaningful exchange of information with our loved ones in spirit. And they don't give us direct access to the ethereals who support our world and our lives in the most incredible ways – access that someday soon, as soon as we on Earth get our affairs in order, will allow wisdom of the ages to stream into our world unfettered by human preconceptions. I hope to see that day in my lifetime, but if I don't, at least I can help plant the seeds before I enter my own probable next phase of ITC – building bridges from the other side of the veil.

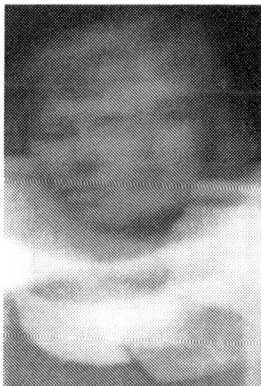

*Of the many hundreds of spirit faces I've gathered on Polaroid film, this is my personal favorite. I took a picture of Joy Schilling of Colorado Springs, and the face of late pop singer John Denver appeared when the photo had developed a few minutes later.*

*Meme posed for several pictures, and in one two spirit faces replaced hers. This one was used on the book cover.*

**MARK MACY** is the author of *Spirit Faces; Truth about the Afterlife*, which consolidates the best of what he's learned about ITC and the afterlife. He has two websites: <www.worlditc.org>, a rather massive site which takes a broad look at ITC efforts around the world, and <www.spiritfaces.com>, which narrows in on his own research. He also worked with The Monroe Institute in Faber, VA, to produce a guided visualization CD called *Bridge to Paradise* that fosters inner work for the specific purpose of opening ITC bridges.